Summary of Contents

BUILD YOUR OWN WICKED WORDPRESS THEMES

BY **ALLAN COLE**
RAENA JACKSON ARMITAGE
BRANDON R. JONES
JEFFREY WAY

Build Your Own Wicked WordPress Themes

by Allan Cole, Raena Jackson Armitage, Brandon R. Jones, and Jeffrey Way

Program Director: Andrew Tetlaw

Technical Editor: Louis Simoneau

Chief Technical Officer: Kevin Yank

Printing History:

　　First Edition: August 2010

Indexer: Fred Brown

Editor: Kelly Steele

Cover Design: Alex Walker

Published by SitePoint Pty. Ltd.

48 Cambridge Street Collingwood
VIC Australia 3066
Web: www.sitepoint.com
Email: business@sitepoint.com

ISBN 978-0-9804552-9-8
Printed and bound in Canada

About Allan Cole

Allan Cole is a web designer and developer based in Brooklyn, NY. He specializes in front-end user experience and WordPress customization. Allan is currently developing a small business rooted in custom WordPress design and development called fthrwght (Feather Weight, http://fthrwght.com/). He can be found online at his portfolio site (http://temp.fthrwght.com/) and his WordPress blog (http://allancole.com/wordpress/).

About Raena Jackson Armitage

Raena Jackson Armitage is an Australian web developer with a background in content management, public speaking, and training. When she's not thinking about the Web, she loves knitting, gaming, all-day breakfasts, and cycling. Raena's personal website is at http://raena.net.

About Brandon R. Jones

From sunny Southern California, Brandon Jones has been designing, drawing, photographing, and coding the world around him for the past several years. Not content to pick one media and stick with it, Brandon has a broad range of talents that have allowed him to work on projects ranging from grungy digital art kits to Fortune 500 software prototyping.

With a strong background in graphic design, digital illustration, and user interface design (as well as a smattering of front-end programming languages), Brandon has enjoyed working with a variety of award-winning studios through his young career. He has a degree from California Polytechnic University at Pomona in Graphic Design, but counts himself as a largely self-taught and self-motivated designer with a desire to play a larger role in the design community. His personal site can be found at http://makedesignnotwar.com/.

About Jeffrey Way

Jeffrey Way works for Envato, where he manages a code marketplace called CodeCanyon, and runs a popular web development tutorial site, Nettuts+. He spends a lot of his free time writing, most recently with the release of *Photoshop to HTML* (http://rockablepress.com/books/photoshop-to-html/). Beyond code, Jeffrey loves to play guitar and embarrass his wife-in-training, Allie, by playing Steel Dragon songs loudly with the windows rolled down in front of movie theaters. You can stop by his website and say hi at www.jeffrey-way.com.

About the Technical Editor

Louis Simoneau joined SitePoint in 2009, after traveling from his native Montréal to Calgary, Taipei, and finally Melbourne. He now gets to spend his days learning about cool web technologies, an activity that had previously been relegated to nights and weekends. He enjoys hip-hop, spicy food, and all things geeky. His personal website is http://louissimoneau.com/ and his latest blog project is http://growbuycookeat.com/.

About the Chief Technical Officer

As Chief Technical Officer for SitePoint, Kevin Yank keeps abreast of all that is new and exciting in web technology. Best known for his book, *Build Your Own Database Driven Web Site Using PHP & MySQL*, he also co-authored *Simply JavaScript* with Cameron Adams and *Everything You Know About CSS Is Wrong!* with Rachel Andrew. In addition, Kevin hosts the *SitePoint Podcast* and co-writes the *SitePoint Tech Times*, a free email newsletter that goes out to over 240,000 subscribers worldwide.

Kevin lives in Melbourne, Australia and enjoys speaking at conferences, as well as visiting friends and family in Canada. He's also passionate about performing improvised comedy theater with Impro Melbourne (http://www.impromelbourne.com.au/) and flying light aircraft. Kevin's personal blog is *Yes, I'm Canadian* (http://yesimcanadian.com/).

About SitePoint

SitePoint specializes in publishing fun, practical, and easy-to-understand content for Web professionals. Visit http://www.sitepoint.com/ to access our blogs, books, newsletters, articles, and community forums.

Special Thanks

Skate gear used in the cover shot is courtesy of Jetty Surf, Greensborough.

Table of Contents

Preface

WordPress is easily the most widely used blogging platform on the Web. Even more impressively, it managed to reach this point in only six years—though, to be fair, that's a lifetime in the Web world! Thanks to a thriving and vibrant community, WordPress has blossomed from a fork of an old blogging platform, called b2, into an easy-to-use, frequently updated, and highly extensible framework.

While years ago it wasn't uncommon to spend hundreds of dollars on a powerful content management system, WordPress is 100% free for everyone. What's more, it's open source, licensed under the General Public License (GPL).

You'll be happy to hear that, assuming you have a modest understanding of PHP, building your first WordPress theme is really quite easy—joyfully easy, in fact! With such ease, one might assume incorrectly that the level of flexibility or power provided by WordPress is lacking. Luckily, this is far from true. Though it might have initially been created specifically for blogging applications, WordPress's power has since been harnessed by talented designers and developers, building everything from forums to ecommerce applications. WordPress is only limited by our imaginations and skill sets, thanks to a powerful and flexible plugin infrastructure.

For web designers, learning how to develop for WordPress opens up enormous opportunities. On one hand, you'll be able to provide clients with dynamic sites that are robust and easy to update at a fraction of what it might cost for an enterprise content management system (CMS). On the other hand, you'll also have the skills to develop general purpose themes for sale on the Web. The market in ready-made WordPress themes has exploded in recent years, so why not get in on the action?

Who Should Read This Book

This book is aimed at front-end web designers looking to branch out from building static sites or simple PHP-based projects into the world of WordPress theme development.

You should already have at least intermediate knowledge of HTML and CSS, as those technologies are as important to WordPress themes as they are to static websites. We'll also assume that you know a little bit of PHP; while there's no requirement for you to be a programming whiz, you should at least understand concepts such as `if` statements, loops, functions and variables, and the way PHP generates HTML for output. While you can certainly customize a theme without using any PHP, the more advanced features shown in the second half of the book require some familiarity with these basics.

What's in This Book

By the end of this book, you'll be able to build attractive, versatile, and powerful WordPress themes. You'll also have a good understanding of what makes a theme successful and how to market your themes effectively.

This book comprises the following eight chapters. You can read them from beginning to end to gain a complete understanding of the subject, or skip around if you only need a refresher on a particular topic.

Chapter 1: *Introducing WordPress*

Before we dive into learning all the ins and outs of designing and building your theme, we'll have a quick look at what exactly WordPress is and what it's made of. We'll also cover why you'd want to be a theme designer in the first place.

Chapter 2: *Planning Your Theme*

To build a truly effective theme, you must understand the needs of the people who'll be using it: both those visiting the site, and those publishing the content. Brandon R. Jones, developer of several of the Web's hottest-selling themes, will walk you through what you should consider before you even start your design.

Chapter 3: *Theme Design 101*

Building on the previous chapter, Brandon now takes you into the design phase in earnest. He'll show you every aspect of a WordPress theme that you need to consider in your designs, with a gallery of the best examples from the Web to serve as inspiration.

Chapter 4: *Theme Frameworks*

In recent years, WordPress theme frameworks have burst onto the scene; they're now considered the best way to build powerful themes quickly without having to rewrite the same template files over and over. In this chapter, WordPress nut Raena Jackson Armitage presents all the reasons you should be using a framework, walks you through some of the most popular options, and introduces you to the one we'll be using for the rest of the book: Thematic.

Chapter 5: *Advanced Theme Construction*

A WordPress theme's greatness is more than skin-deep. In this chapter, Raena takes you beyond simple CSS skinning and shows you how to bend WordPress's markup to your will, thanks to Thematic's array of hooks, filters, and templates.

Chapter 6: *Widgets*

One of WordPress's killer features is its widget functionality, which provides users with the ability to easily add dynamic content to various areas in the site. In this chapter, Thematic expert Allan Cole shows you how to make your theme widget-ready, as well as how to create your own custom widgets to package with it.

Chapter 7: *Theme Options*

The most successful themes on the market allow users to fully customize them to suit a site's purpose. Whether it's creating a custom options page to allow users to modify your theme's behavior, adding color and layout variants, providing alternative page templates, or developing your own custom shortcodes, Allan will show you how to turn your theme into a veritable chameleon.

Chapter 8: *Selling Your Themes*

As site manager of the Web's largest WordPress theme marketplace, Jeffrey Way knows a thing or two about what makes WordPress themes fly off the proverbial—and virtual—shelves. In this chapter, he'll give you the secrets that will help take your themes to the top of the charts.

Where to Find Help

SitePoint has a thriving community of web designers and developers ready and waiting to help you out if you run into trouble. We also maintain a list of known errata for this book, which you can consult for the latest updates; the details follow.

The SitePoint Forums

The SitePoint Forums[1] are discussion forums where you can ask questions about anything related to web development. You may, of course, answer questions too. That's how a discussion forum site works—some people ask, some people answer, and most people do a bit of both. Sharing your knowledge benefits others and strengthens the community. A lot of interesting and experienced web designers and developers hang out there. It's a good way to learn new stuff, have questions answered in a hurry, and have a blast.

The Book's Website

Located at http://www.sitepoint.com/books/wordpress1/, the website that supports this book will give you access to the following facilities.

The Code Archive

As you progress through this book, you'll note a number of references to the code archive. This is a downloadable ZIP archive that contains every line of example source code that's printed in this book, as well as other supporting documents. If you want to cheat (or save yourself from carpal tunnel syndrome), go ahead and download the archive.[2]

---

[1] http://www.sitepoint.com/forums/
[2] http://www.sitepoint.com/books/wordpress1/code.php

Updates and Errata

No book is perfect, and we expect that watchful readers will be able to spot at least one or two mistakes before the end of this one. The Errata page[3] on the book's website will always have the latest information about known typographical and code errors.

The SitePoint Newsletters

In addition to books like this one, SitePoint publishes free email newsletters, such as the *SitePoint Tech Times*, *SitePoint Tribune*, and *SitePoint Design View*, to name a few. In them, you'll read about the latest news, product releases, trends, tips, and techniques for all aspects of web development. Sign up to one or more SitePoint newsletters at http://www.sitepoint.com/newsletter/.

The SitePoint Podcast

Join the SitePoint Podcast team for news, interviews, opinion, and fresh thinking for web developers and designers. We discuss the latest web industry topics, present guest speakers, and interview some of the best minds in the industry. You can catch up on the latest and previous podcasts at http://www.sitepoint.com/podcast/, or subscribe via iTunes.

Your Feedback

If you're unable to find an answer through the forums, or if you wish to contact us for any other reason, the best place to write is books@sitepoint.com. We have a well-staffed email support system set up to track your inquiries, and if our support team members are unable to answer your question, they'll send it straight to us. Suggestions for improvements, as well as notices of any mistakes you may find, are especially welcome.

Acknowledgments

Raena Jackson Armitage

First, thanks to everyone at SitePoint—but especially Andrew, Louis, Kelly, Georgina, and Shayne, all of whom played their part to whip my stuff into shape and make it all sound more smart. Thanks also to Lukas and Cindy and everyone on Jarrett Street; to Mathew and Tim for being encouraging; to Avi, Beth, Dan, Donna, Ed, Karl, Dr. Mike, and to everyone who encouraged a curious, timid chick to take IT seriously as a career.

---

[3] http://www.sitepoint.com/books/wordpress1/errata.php

Allan Cole

First, I'd like to thank Louis Simoneau and the rest of the SitePoint guys for being patient and understanding with deadlines. I know it must be tough to coordinate and put all of this together. I'd like to thank my friend Adria Richards for inspiring me to get out of my comfort zone and do something out of the norm. She also helped out with a bit of proofreading early on, which was greatly appreciated. Thanks to Ashley Moore-Motte and Sabrina Smith, for their tips on writing a whole lot in a little amount of time. Thanks to Ian Stewart as well for providing such an easy way for WordPress geeks like myself to learn and share code with the community. Lastly, a great deal of thanks goes out to my parents, Jeff and Rese Cole; Darien Birks, Lawrence Atoigue, and the rest of my Brooklyn and Maryland/Washington family for their continued support in all of my endeavors.

Brandon R. Jones

Thanks to the WordPress core development group: without you guys and gals, none of this would even be possible. Thanks also to Jeffrey Way and the entire Envato staff; the awesome authors at ThemeForest; Nettuts; WooThemes; the Shane & Peter Inc. crew; all the awesome designers and developers whose work was included in this book; and everyone else working to make the Web an open and altogether wonderful place to work.

Jeffrey Way

Had it not been for the massive schooling that I received after being hired by Envato in 2008, I would never have been afforded the skill set, let alone the opportunity, to write for SitePoint. I will be forever grateful to Collis Ta'eed, Cyan Ta'eed, Skellie, and Jason Ellis for teaching me as much as they have. Secondly, I learned a great deal from a large number of fantastic web designers on ThemeForest.net, who taught me exactly what it takes to be a successful and profitable WordPress coder. Many of their tricks and techniques have made their way into the last chapter of this book.

Conventions Used in This Book

You'll notice that we've used certain typographic and layout styles throughout the book to signify different types of information. Look out for the following items.

Code Samples

Code in this book will be displayed using a fixed-width font, like so:

```
<h1>A Perfect Summer's Day</h1>
<p>It was a lovely day for a walk in the park. The birds
were singing and the kids were all back at school.</p>
```

If the code is to be found in the book's code archive, the name of the file will appear at the top of the program listing, like this:

```
                                                                    example.css
.footer {
  background-color: #CCC;
  border-top: 1px solid #333;
}
```

If only part of the file is displayed, this is indicated by the word *excerpt*:

```
                                                            example.css (excerpt)
  border-top: 1px solid #333;
```

If additional code is to be inserted into an existing example, the new code will be displayed in bold:

```
function animate() {
  new_variable = "Hello";
}
```

Where existing code is required for context, rather than repeat all the code, a vertical ellipsis will be displayed:

```
function animate() {
  ⋮
  return new_variable;
}
```

Some lines of code are intended to be entered on one line, but we've had to wrap them because of page constraints. A ➥ indicates a line break that exists for formatting purposes only, and should be ignored:

```
URL.open("http://www.sitepoint.com/blogs/2007/05/28/user-style-she
➥ets-come-of-age/");
```

Tips, Notes, and Warnings

Hey, You!

Tips will give you helpful little pointers.

Ahem, Excuse Me ...

Notes are useful asides that are related—but not critical—to the topic at hand. Think of them as extra tidbits of information.

Make Sure You Always ...

... pay attention to these important points.

Watch Out!

Warnings will highlight any gotchas that are likely to trip you up along the way.

Introducing WordPress

by Jeffrey Way

So, you've been messing about with websites for a little while now, and you've decided to take the plunge and learn how to design themes for WordPress. Perhaps you're a blogger yourself, and you want to take the next step by redesigning your site, or perhaps you've heard that there's a strong market for ready-made WordPress themes and you want to get in on the ground floor, so to speak. You're probably itching to start building your first WordPress theme, but before we jump in, it's a good idea to think about why we're here, and how we arrived. This chapter will give you a bit of background on WordPress in general and WordPress themes in particular.

In the following two chapters Brandon will take you through the process of planning and designing your theme; then Raena will take over and introduce you to the code behind WordPress themes and the Thematic framework, which will make your life as a developer much more enjoyable. After that, Allan will take you through the slightly more advanced topics of widgets and custom theme options; and finally, it's me again, Jeffrey, back to provide some insight into how to sell your themes and profit from them.

Here we go!

A Brief History of WordPress

Many of you may be unaware that WordPress is based on a blogging platform with a modest adoption rate—a few thousand installations—built in mid-2001 and called b2.[1] Michel Valdrighi, its developer, managed development for roughly two years before the platform's users began to notice that he'd seemingly abandoned the project. Fortunately for thousands upon thousands of loyal WordPress users, one particular b2 fan was Matt Mullenweg, the creator of WordPress.

Thanks to the convenience of online archives, we can trace the inception of WordPress back to one single blog entry,[2] made by Mullenweg on January 24th, 2003:

> […] My logging software [b2] hasn't been updated for months, and the main developer has disappeared, and I can only hope that he's okay.
>
> What to do? Well, Textpattern looks like everything I could ever want, but it doesn't look like it's going to be licensed under something politically I could agree with. Fortunately, b2/cafelog is GPL, which means that I could use the existing codebase to create a fork, integrating all the cool stuff that Michel would be working on right now if only he was around. The work would never be lost, as if I fell of the face of the planet a year from now, whatever code I made would be free to the world, and if someone else wanted to pick it up they could. I've decided that this the course of action I'd like to go in, now all I need is a name. What should it do? Well, it would be nice to have the flexibility of MovableType (sic), the parsing of TextPattern (sic), the hackability of b2, and the ease of setup of Blogger. Someday, right?
>
> —Matt Mullenweg

This date marks WordPress's birthday—at least in hindsight! In that short two-paragraph posting, called "The Blogging Software Dilemma," Matt sows the seed of an idea that will eventually turn into WordPress. Over the course of 2003, along with Mike Little, Matt did indeed fork b2 and prepare the first release of WordPress, which ultimately was announced on December 26th.

WordPress Today

If we leap forward six years, WordPress has now been installed over 22 million times, easily making it the most popular blogging platform in the world. Due to its extensibility, literally thousands of plugins have been built on top of the framework, allowing for increased functionality, including the handling of sites like job boards and wikis. And, most importantly for us, thousands of themes have been developed to give WordPress nearly any look imaginable.

---

[1] http://www.cafelog.com
[2] http://ma.tt/2003/01/the-blogging-software-dilemma/

Matt has since formed Automattic—WordPress's parent company—and has been named one of the 50 most important people on the Web[3] by *PC World*.

WordPress is currently supported by roughly a dozen core developers, and a plethora of active contributors in the community, including the creator of b2, Michel Valdrighi.

Why WordPress?

Despite all that horn blowing, why choose WordPress over the array of other excellent blogging platforms and CMSes available around the Web, including Movable Type and Blogger? Surely they have an equal number of impressive stats to spout, right? Well, you might choose WordPress for a variety of reasons:

- It's free. Whether you're building a simple personal blog, or a high-level business website for a Fortune 500 company, working with WordPress will cost you nothing.

- The original b2 framework was licensed under the **GPL** (General Public License), and so is WordPress. The GPL allows developers the freedom to modify and redistribute the software, as long as you provide others the same freedoms. This brings several advantages, including WordPress being actively developed by its community as well as the core WordPress team.

- It's known for its incredibly simple 5-Minute Install.[4]

- There is an enormous number of WordPress resources available on the Web, including free themes and a large number of both written and video tutorials.

- The WordPress documentation—called the Codex[5]—is second to none.

- WordPress has been around for seven years, so we can rest assured that it's here to stay, and will continue to be actively developed for years to come.

- The WordPress team organizes community meetups, as well as conferences called WordCamps. The meetups are more casual in nature, and generally consist of team and community members talking about everything from new features in the latest version of WordPress, to tips and tricks. WordCamps consist of lectures from both core developers and community members. To learn more, visit http://central.wordcamp.org/.

As with any technology choice, the decision to use WordPress ultimately comes down to personal preference. But with all those reasons, and a platform that's continually growing in popularity, it's really more a question of, "Why *wouldn't* you use WordPress?"

---

[3] http://www.pcworld.com/article/129301/the_50_most_important_people_on_the_web.html

[4] http://codex.wordpress.org/Installing_WordPress#Famous_5-Minute_Install

[5] http:// codex.wordpress.org/

WordPress.com and WordPress.org

If you're entirely new to WordPress, the difference between wordpress.org and wordpress.com and might be a bit confusing at first. The first site, wordpress.org, is the home of the free and open source WordPress software platform. If your intention is to develop custom themes and host the CMS on your own server, wordpress.org is the only option.

WordPress.com, meanwhile, is a commercial entity operated by Automattic, which provides hosted blogging using the WordPress platform. It's free to use, though there are a number of premium features available for a fee.

Here are the pros and cons of each:

WordPress.org pros
- access to thousands of custom themes
- use of custom widgets and plugins
- retention of 100% control over the markup
- access to the MySQL database, should you need to make revisions or create new tables

WordPress.org cons
- responsible for acquiring your own hosting, at a cost
- manual installation of software required
- download required of necessary plugins to prevent spam (typically Automattic's popular Akismet plugin)

WordPress.com pros
- hosted and managed by Automattic for free
- hosted on hundreds of servers, resulting in virtually 99% uptime
- set up, comment spam, and database back ups performed automatically for free

WordPress.com cons
- limited access to themes (around 100), and custom themes not permitted
- unable to modify underlying PHP code
- custom plugins can't be implemented
- initial listing as a subdomain of wordpress.com, such as mysite.wordpress.com, though it's possible to map your own domain address to this URL

For the purposes of this book, you'll need to use the software downloaded from wordpress.org, and installed either on your desktop computer, web server, or virtual machine. Head over to wordpress.org and download the latest version[6] (3.0 at the time of writing), then install it according to the instructions on the Codex.[7]

What is a Theme?

Don't confuse the content—the pages and posts—with the theme; they're unrelated. In fact, this separation is what makes WordPress and theming so powerful!

WordPress is a framework that provides all of the functionality for RSS, commenting, searching, querying the database, displaying posts, creating pages, and the like. The theme, on the other hand, is the skin: how it looks, the layout of the design, the CSS, added functionality, and images. Because each theme hooks into WordPress's core functions and filters in the same way, you can switch between themes with a click of a button. Any WordPress-powered site can instantly don your theme and rock a whole new look.

Each theme resides within a subdirectory of your WordPress installation called **themes**. If some new theme—like the one we'll start building in Chapter 5—is called "Wicked," it can be found within **wp-content/themes/wicked**. This separation of the presentation from the system files is incredibly helpful; it makes future updates to the WordPress framework easy, since you can update the core WordPress files without changing the theme.

Themes are essentially divided into three components:

Presentation

A file called **style.css** contains all the style rules that will be applied to your theme.

Content

Template files describe what content should be output on each of WordPress's pages: lists of posts, single posts, search results, and so on.

Logic

A file called **functions.php** contains any additional logic your theme needs in order to, well, *function*. As we'll see in later chapters, this is where you'd include plugin-like functionality in your theme: new custom widgets, or a theme-specific admin panel for customizing the color scheme and layout.

This file is immediately loaded during WordPress's initialization, and can also be modified to define common functions that are used throughout your theme.

When you download and install WordPress, you're presented with the base framework, and the default theme Twenty Ten, shown in Figure 1.1.

---

[6] http://wordpress.org/download/
[7] http://codex.wordpress.org/Installing_WordPress

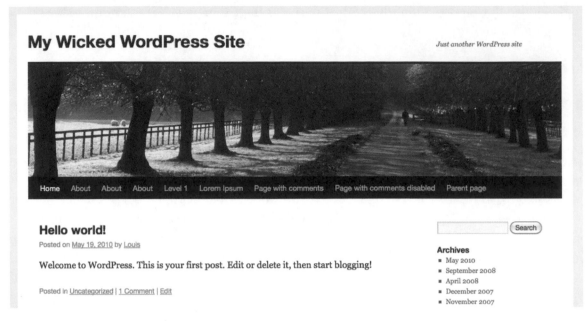

Figure 1.1. The default WordPress theme, Twenty Ten

Visiting your site's theme administration page (from the Dashboard, click **Appearance**, then **Themes**), you'll see a selection of all the themes you've installed—or just the default one if you've yet to install any—and you can activate any of them by clicking the **Activate** link. To test out a few different themes and get a feel for how they modify the site's appearance, select the **Install Themes** tab and grab yourself some new ones. You'll see how completely they can change the blog's look, but you might also start to think of ways they could be improved, or of the kind of theme you'd like to build. Perfect!

Why become a WordPress theme designer?

Well, you've already purchased this book, so it goes without saying that you want to become one! However, if you're still on the fence, it might be beneficial to ask yourself: "What do I want out of WordPress?" Do you hate the idea of using another designer's theme on your site? Did you find that none of the currently available themes suit the needs of your blog or business? Those are both great reasons to learn how to build your own theme. Some others might include being able to:

- customize existing themes
- convert your own website designs into WordPress templates
- sell your theme designs for profit
- add WordPress theme design to your agency's services
- give back to the community with unique designs

If you identify with any of these reasons, it makes perfect sense to dive head-first into WordPress theme design. Fortunately for you, the learning curve is quite reasonable.

If your ultimate goal is to turn this into a business, it can be a lucrative one if you play your cards right. Some theme authors on ThemeForest[8]—the theme marketplace site I manage—make over $25,000 every single month! Of course, it takes time to build up your catalog, but once you do, automation and the compound effects of selling multiple themes will yield returns, as sales roll in every day without any additional effort on your part.

And Finally ...

There's a reason why over 20 million people have installed WordPress: it's easy, free, extensible, themeable, profitable, and, most importantly, fun to use. As a web designer, you already have many of the skills required to build your own wicked WordPress themes. So let's do it!

---

[8] http://themeforest.net/

Chapter 2

Planning Your Theme

by Brandon R. Jones

Before you even fire up Photoshop or your favorite code editor, it's important to define some goals for the WordPress theme that you'll be building. What function will it serve for its visitors? How should it assist the content authors or publishers who'll be using it? Answering these questions early on will save time, energy, and money in the long run.

This chapter will help to refine your vision for a theme into a lean, mean, focused set of directives, becoming your personal road map during the design process (which we'll jump into in the next chapter).

Once you've designed a WordPress theme, there's a lot that will be out of your control. Individual authors will use your theme in ways that are impossible to predict. Visitors will demand features that you never even considered, or be confused by features that you thought would be useful. Sure, you can release updates to your theme to take in those requests and suggestions, but establishing a strategy for your theme ahead of time will, at the very least, give you a set of ground rules for what your theme should attempt to do.

In a way, this is part of the particular challenge and excitement of designing a WordPress theme. The best that you can do is come up with a clear vision of what you want the theme to be, and design with that ideal in mind. At the same time, you should always remember that what you're building is a tool that others will adapt and bend to their purposes.

What do you start with?

Before you start planning your custom WordPress theme, it's a good idea to familiarize yourself with the default structure and hierarchy of a WordPress site. By acquainting yourself with all its components, you'll be better positioned to decide how you want to organize them in your theme, in a way that distinguishes it from a vanilla installation. If you've worked with WordPress in the past and are already familiar with its parts, you can most likely skip this section and go straight to the section called "Defining Success".

At its core, WordPress is a blogging engine, so the default home page shows a list of recent posts. From there, users can navigate to pages that list posts by category, tag (we'll go over the difference between tags and categories shortly), or month (these monthly listing pages are called **archives** in WordPress). You can also click on the title of a post to reach its page, along with a list of comments and a form to post a new comment. WordPress also accommodates static pages that can exist in a hierarchy; for example, a given site might have an About page, with child pages called Contact Us and Our Staff.

Of course, this default structure can be customized endlessly, but by understanding what you start with, you'll know what needs changing and what should be kept.

Let's go over each of these components in a bit more detail.

Pages and Posts

Pages and posts are the two main types of content that you'll find in a WordPress theme.

Posts are the bread and butter of the WordPress theme. You can have as many of them as you want, and they're usually listed in reverse chronological order on blog list pages. Generally, posts are published periodically and used for any kind of timely content such as news items, blog entries, episodes of a podcast, stories, and so on.

WordPress **pages** are different from posts, in that they are static and not date-sensitive. Authors usually use pages for content like About information or Contact Us. A theme can have as many pages as the author wishes, and publishers can even use subpages to establish page hierarchy; however, the majority of sites use only a handful of top-level pages at most. The exception is a business site that uses WordPress as a CMS (content management system) rather than a blogging engine.

Media and Links

In addition to pages and blog posts, WordPress allows publishers to create two other forms of content: media and links. **Links** are just that: hyperlinks pointing to other pages on the Internet. Traditionally, this functionality was used to allow bloggers to maintain a **blogroll**—that is, a list of other blogs they enjoyed.

Media refers to any types of images, audio files, and video files that are uploaded to a WordPress site, and can subsequently be used in pages or blog posts.

The default handling of media and links is quite satisfactory for many sites. When you reach the design phase, though, you'll need to consider how different types of media are displayed and keep them consistent with the rest of the theme's visual feel.

Custom Fields

WordPress also allows authors to add **custom fields** to their posts. For example, on a movie review site, the content publisher might assign a rating to each movie in addition to the review itself. Then, all the publisher need do is enter a key ("Rating") and a value ("3 stars") into the custom fields when creating their post.

Your theme might not rely heavily on custom fields, but you need to at least plan for their possible presence for the sake of design consistency. That said, if you're designing a special-purpose theme, you can use custom fields as a way to implement a given feature.

Categories and Tags

Posts are the primary content type of most WordPress sites, and are usually quite numerous. As a result, WordPress includes a few features to help publishers organize posts, making them easier for readers to find.

Categories are a hierarchical method of organizing the site's posts. For instance, if you have a site that offers reviews on automobiles, your categories would likely include "Cars," "Trucks," "Motorcycles," and "Recreational Vehicles." You can have subcategories as well; hence, under "Cars," you might have "Sedans," "Luxury," "Sports," and "Hybrids." An author can assign a post to any number of categories.

Tags are a way of attaching keywords to blog posts. Unlike categories, tags aren't organized into any sort of hierarchy. Essentially, they allow you to be more granular in your classification of content. Using the previous example, a post could be filed under the category of "Cars," and then be tagged with "Blue," "Sunroof," and "V8."

As a general rule of thumb: categories *organize* content, while tags *label* content.

Any WordPress theme should enable content publishers to use either method of organization, and should make allowances for both in the theme design.

Comments

A key component of most blogs is a comment system for visitors to leave messages about the posts they view. Usually pages that contain a single post feature a list of posted comments and a comment form. In multiple-post pages (such as the home page, or a category or archive listing), often what's shown is just the number of comments the post has received.

Comments can also be **threaded**, which means a comment can be posted *in reply* to a previous one. This is usually indicated visually by having the reply indented below the comment it addresses, though you can come up with your own way of representing it.

Widgets

WordPress also allows publishers to easily add and arrange sidebar content using **widgets**. The most recent versions of WordPress include drag and drop interfaces that allow authors to simply configure the different types of content that should be shown in each sidebar. Let's take a peek at what this interface looks like in WordPress 3.0, shown in Figure 2.1.

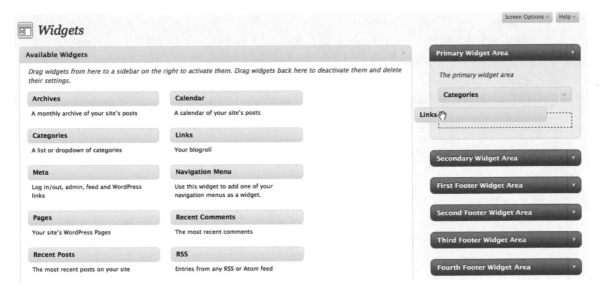

Figure 2.1. The widget interface in WordPress

A good WordPress theme should enable publishers to use as many widgets as they want, and include them in a number of areas on the site without breaking the theme's style or layout. This allows for more flexibility and increases the value a blogger gains from the theme. We'll go into much more detail about how to include custom widgets and prepare sections of your theme for widgets in Chapter 6; in the meantime, just remember that some parts of your pages should be reserved for widget placement.

The Loop

Pages in your theme that display blog posts—for example, a page which lists all posts in a given category, or all posts published in a certain month—rely on a feature of WordPress called **The Loop**. It's one of the most important parts of a template—such a big deal, in fact, that WordPress geeks like to capitalize its name. We'll be covering this in a lot more detail in Chapter 5; for now, all you need to know is that by default, posts are always displayed using this mechanism in essentially the same way. This is, of course, infinitely customizable, but the default behavior is that simple. It's called The Loop because WordPress loops through all the blog posts that are to be displayed, and renders each one the same way.

Menus

WordPress 3.0 added support for user-defined menus, making WordPress even more powerful as a CMS. Users can create their own menus, made up of pages, categories, or any other links they'd like. They can also reorder the menu items at a whim. Your theme can even include multiple different menu locations, in the same way that you can include multiple widget areas, to allow your users even more control over their site's navigation.

Allan will be showing you how to take advantage of custom menus in your theme in Chapter 7, but it's worth keeping in mind that your users will potentially have full control over the site's navigation. This means that you're unable to depend on a fixed number of links or menu items, so your design has to be flexible.

Now that you know what a WordPress theme comprises, it's time to start thinking about *your* theme, and how you want it to look and act.

Defining Success

WordPress is an incredibly flexible platform to design for. As a theme designer and developer, you have a range of available options: you can include all kinds of JavaScript wizardry, spend hours on typographic minutiae, or include a raft of custom options for your users. As a result, designing WordPress themes is as much about deciding what to leave out as what to put in. And this can be difficult to do if you lack a strong vision of the purpose that sites using your theme will serve to their visitors.

Because of this, your first job as a theme designer is to think about what you want your theme to accomplish. What will it take for your theme to be successful? What characteristics should your completed theme possess?

Defining success can be as simple as a making a statement about your intentions for the theme. It might look like any of these:

- "My theme will focus on delivering a new and exciting layout for blogs with text-driven content."

- "I want to build a theme that allows photographers to display their images in a sleek, minimal design."

- "Our goal is to develop a theme for video-based sites with a built-in collection of robust sharing tools."

■ "The purpose of this theme is to offer a simple template for small business websites."

What would be the definition of success for your particular WordPress theme? If you're unable to explain in one brief statement what your theme's goals are, the design process will be like throwing darts in the dark.

The beautiful thing about declaring a mission statement for your WordPress theme is that when you're confronted with a difficult design decision later on, you can always go back to that statement to help you out.

For example, imagine that you're trying to decide whether to include a cool new image slider for your theme. If your mission statement was the first one I listed before, chances are good that it's unnecessary, unless you can prove that people are going to need it. Most bloggers using your theme will probably be more interested in making it easy for their visitors to find the content they're looking for. Moreover, because these posts are unlikely to include images, devoting your design and development time to such a feature is a bad idea.

No matter how complex your design or coding challenges become in the later phases, your mission statement should be the guiding light that everything should follow.

Planning Milestone

■ What is the mission statement for your theme?

Letting Your Content Lead the Way

Selecting the type of content that your theme will focus on is no superficial decision; it will play a significant role in the design decisions you make, and the features you choose to include. For the most part, you can let your content do the work for you. Planning a set of features to complement your content is as easy as letting that content shine.

There is an extensive variety of content types available, with an even larger number of hybrids that exist. Using the four sample mission statements we outlined in the last section, here are the content types each one will primarily serve:

The Blog Theme
The classic blog archetype that WordPress was modeled on is built around text content that's frequently updated. Visitors to this type of site want to access the content that they're after easily. This could be articles, tutorials, journals, reviews, or any other form that primarily uses text to communicate. Authors will pick a text-based theme because it makes it easy to publish their writing, and because it makes it easy for their readers to find the content they're looking for.

With this theme, the typography itself becomes a key feature: big, juicy, readable text is more than a luxury—it's essential to the theme's success in meeting the demands of its viewers. Text-driven themes often carry a lot of blog posts as well, so it would be worth considering various methods that allow users to find relevant content. We'll discuss organization in more depth later on in this chapter.

The Image-centric Theme

Photographers, design studios, illustrators, and image-rich magazines are just some of the types of businesses that want to publish content that's centered around images. Visitors are likely to come to these sites for large, attractive images, and for the tools that make it easy to browse these images. Authors will generally pick a theme that caters towards this kind of content, giving images a lot of prominence in the layout.

An image-centric theme needs to consider the size of the main content column, as this determines the maximum width of images. It's also important to contemplate image-relevant features such as a lightbox, an image gallery template, custom thumbnails, and an image slider on the front page.

The Video Site Theme

Video is an increasingly popular medium for delivering content on the Web. In many ways, the design goals and constraints of a video theme will be similar to those of an image-centric theme, though you'll have the benefit of a more consistent content size and shape to design for. Your typical site visitor will appreciate the ability to share videos easily with their friends, and publishers seek easy support for a number of popular embedded video players.

The video blog will need a customized layout and feature set to suit the needs of the video content. The layout must make the activity of watching the videos as easy as possible. Give some thought to where the video player (or players) will be located in the layout. Allowing visitors the ability to easily browse for similar videos would be a great feature. Social media sharing links should be easy to access as well, so that visitors can share the videos with their friends directly.

The Business Site Theme

Though initially developed as a blogging platform, WordPress is also very well-suited to being used as a content management system for a business or other promotional website. As businesses recognize the importance of integrating powerful content management and social media tools into their websites, this type of WordPress-based site will only become more prevalent. Content on this kind of site will include About and Contact pages, though there should also be good support for blog or news content.

When it comes to this form of theme, ease of customization and branding is crucial, as the company will want to ensure the site reflects its professional identity. Key features often include highly customizable colors, space reserved for a bold mission statement on the home page, and plenty of ways to organize a firm's core business content into a form that more closely resembles a printed brochure than your standard text blog.

Of course, most customers will be looking to publish a mix of content types. For example, a small photography studio might be looking for a theme that makes it simple to create attractive static pages, in addition to the features common to image-centric themes, like galleries or sliders. Bloggers usually want the ability to easily include images or videos in their posts, while many businesses want to have blog content on their sites. Given these variations, having a good idea of the primary content type your theme aims to deliver will enable you to give such content particular prominence, and make your job easier when selecting features for your theme.

In each of these four examples, the key point to remember is that we're letting the content do the planning for us. You can always add or remove features based on your unique take on the archetype later on. At this point in the planning process, you should start by creating a bare-bones list of features that are essential to the content type and mission statement.

Planning Milestone

- What is your theme's primary content type?
- Do you need to plan for any other types of content that will be included in the mix?
- What are the key features required to deliver the theme's core content?
- What will the overall design layout look like?

Doing Your Research

Art historians are fond of the saying, "great artists stand upon the shoulders of their predecessors." The same goes for WordPress theme creators. The best themers choose not to start from square one. They look at what's already out there, then add their own unique blend of innovation. As such, doing a little reconnaissance (the military term for scouting out the battlefield) is a crucial part of the design process for a number of reasons:

- It will tell you what's already being done in the field. Nobody wants to spend days crafting a specialized theme only to find a similar offering in existence.

- You'll learn what's missing in the market. Spotting a new type of niche theme or feature that has yet to be built (or hasn't been built *well*) can often result in a blockbuster hit.

- It will tell you what's working and what isn't. Often, themes will have discussion boards attached where you can read users' feedback. Why wait until your theme is done before you start collecting information about how people will use it?

Now that you know why you should do your recon, let's dig in a little deeper.

Theme Research

One of the beautiful aspects about working with WordPress is that there are thousands of themes already in existence: some are great, others less so. Take some time to browse the Web for themes that are similar to what you're trying to accomplish. If you're building a hot new video theme, check out the array of themes that focus on video. There's a good chance that you'll be able to produce a list of the features that you love—as well as features that you hate—and any changes that you'd like to bring to your own personal take on a video theme.

The WordPress theme library[1] has much to offer, but you should also look further afield. Some of the best themes are premium offerings showcased on outside websites. Open up your favorite search engine and begin hunting for themes that share your theme's target market. Once you have a good grasp on the state of affairs for your particular niche, you can start making an educated list of features and design elements to take into the design phase.

Plugin Research

Plugins are another reason why working with WordPress is so much nicer than working with other online publishing platforms. With over ten thousand plugins in the official plugin directory alone, it's hard to come up with an idea that's yet to be implemented in some form. Requiring authors to use outside plugins with your theme is generally a bad idea, since it makes your theme dependent on a third party; in many cases you can replicate the feature behind the plugin and turn it into a fully supported part of your theme. Taking the time to look into any relevant plugins will provide you with a crash course of the existing features that are available. This exercise also provides a veritable treasure trove of feedback since most of these plugins display ratings and comments from users.

Let's look at an example of researching plugins to help you plan a theme. If you were building a photography theme, it follows that you'd search for existing plugins dealing with image-related functionality such as lightboxes and galleries. Here are just three hypothetical ways of using theme research:

- You encounter some ideas that are worth including in your own custom theme. By spending just a short while searching for lightbox plugins, you're able to plan out exactly what you want in your own theme's lightbox.

- You discover that there's no current plugin for a certain feature that you had in mind—so you plan on building it directly into your theme. This enables you to address the functionality that WordPress users might be seeking. Later on you can use this unique feature to promote your theme.

---

[1] http://wordpress.org/extend/themes/

■ You find that the image gallery system that you were going to use is irritating lots of publishers. By making a few adjustments based on this user feedback, you can make it more helpful to publishers.

Script Research

Finally, searching for what's new in the world of JavaScript is often a valuable exercise when hunting for new ways to deliver on your theme's goals. In most cases, there's no need to be an expert in any particular script language to be able to use scripts inside your theme. Most scripts are licensed under the GPL (which means you can distribute them in your theme files[2]), and most are well-documented, so that installing and using them just requires following the provided instructions.

At this point, you should also give some thought to which JavaScript libraries (for example, jQuery or Prototype), if any, your theme will use. Depending on your level of JavaScript proficiency, libraries can make the task of developing custom features and shiny gadgets much easier.

Script research can be a lot of fun, because fancy new effects and features are constantly being developed by the coding community at large. While you do need to ensure that the scripts you include work on all major browsers, in most cases the script authors will have already done the testing for you.

Keep on Scouting

Obviously, there's a great deal of research that can be done beyond the scope of existing themes, plugins, and scripts. You can also hunt for examples of functionality on other platforms, and models of clever design in alternative media (print, movies, and even architecture can be sources of inspiration). The underlying principle behind this exercise is simple: now that you've crystallized the primary goals for your theme, go out and see if there are better ways to implement them than you'd previously anticipated.

Planning Milestone

■ Scout out the Web for new ideas. Make a list of the scripts, plugins, and themes that you like; then go back to your previous feature list and revise as you see fit.

Avoiding Feature Bloat

You may think to yourself, "Why not just design a theme that can handle every conceivable type of content?" Much like an automobile that also tries to be a helicopter, jet boat, and commercial airliner all at once, the idea of the catchall "Swiss Army knife" theme is a dangerous one. By tacking on every feature and design element you can imagine, you end up creating Frankenstein's monster; rather than succeeding at everything, your theme winds up failing to be particularly good at anything.

---

[2] For more on the GPL and its relationship to WordPress themes, see the section called "Understanding the GPL" in Chapter 8.

This type of **feature bloat** can lead to a number of problems in a WordPress theme:

■ Content can become muddled, making it difficult for users to find what they're looking for.

■ Features might cause conflicts with other plugins, leading to frequent bugs or an unreliable layout.

■ Flashy tools might dominate the design, making it hard for publishers to draw attention to their content.

■ The amount of customization options may make it difficult for publishers to use.

Remember, WordPress is supposed to make the lives of authors and visitors easier. If a theme includes too many features, using them on a regular basis becomes cumbersome.

The plain fact is that it's often simpler to pick one type of content at which your theme can excel, and stick to it. If you encounter situations where you absolutely must add a new feature, you can make those decisions on a case-by-case basis, according to your theme's mission statement. There are always good reasons to make exceptions, but sticking to your theme's primary goals when creating your final feature set will ward off feature bloat in the long run.

Designing Based on Content is Different from Supporting It

One important point to note here is that while you should avoid designing a theme that focuses on all conceivable types of content, it's important that you at least *support all types of content*. This might seem like a contradiction, but I assure you I'm not just splitting hairs. *Designing* a theme for all kinds of content is distracting; *supporting* all kinds of content is just good practice. If an author of a text blog decides to include video or images in a post, and your theme's styles look broken or display incorrectly—your theme has failed. It's unnecessary to have a custom template for each and every type of content out there; just ensure that most common forms of media have at least some basic styling support.

Planning Milestone

■ Without detracting from the theme's primary goal, what additional features should your theme include to enhance a visitor's experience?

Planning for the Audience

The people who will visit the sites using your theme are, ultimately, your audience. While it is impossible to predict accurately the type of user who's going to be making use of the content on your themes, it's worth spending some time considering the ideal visitor experience.

This may sound obvious, but you'd be surprised how few theme authors truly think about the ways a visitor will actually interact with their theme. Here are some examples of sites that have anticipated visitor behavior and planned ahead for it with carefully thought-out features:

Nettuts+ (http://net.tutsplus.com/)

> This website caters to web developers by providing step-by-step tutorials. As such, the site includes a lot of code examples where the code from the tutorial is actually shown inside the blog post. In anticipating user behavior, Nettuts+ includes inline code examples in boxes that not only make the text look like code (complete with syntax highlighting), but include buttons for copying the script to the user's clipboard; this makes following the tutorial a seamless experience. A sample code snippet from Nettuts+ is shown in Figure 2.2.

```
   view plain   copy to clipboard   print   ?
1.    .rate_widget {
2.        border:      1px solid #CCC;
3.        overflow:    visible;
4.        padding:     10px;
5.        position:    relative;
6.        width:       180px;
7.        height:      32px;
8.    }
9.    .ratings_stars {
10.       background: url('star_empty.png') no-repeat;
11.       float:       left;
12.       height:      28px;
13.       padding:     2px;
14.       width:       32px;
15.    }
16.    .ratings_vote {
17.       background: url('star_full.png') no-repeat;
18.    }
```

Figure 2.2. Code snippets on the Nettuts+ site

WineLibraryTV (http://tv.winelibrary.com/)

> This website delivers reviews of wine in a style that's both comical and educational. The videos often take 20 to 30 minutes to review a handful of wines; however, the host will usually only spend a few minutes on each particular wine. Because of this, users often like to skip directly to the spot in the video that reviews the wine in which they're interested. As an indicator of good planning, WineLibraryTV uses a video player that allows for bookmarks in the video, so that visitors can instantly find the content they're looking for, as seen in Figure 2.3.

Figure 2.3. Video player on the WineLibraryTV site

Psdtuts+

This website features a lot of content catering to web and graphic designers. Because the audience is web-savvy, many visitors are eager to share its content on social networks that they use. As another good example of preparation, the site owners have built in a social media bar at the bottom of their posts, making information sharing as simple as possible. This example, shown in Figure 2.4, receives bonus points because it also includes a section that helps users find further content.

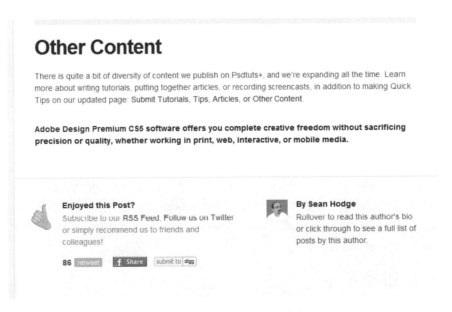

Figure 2.4. The social media buttons on Psdtuts+

Planning for the audience involves more than just anticipating the type of content they seek; it is actively preparing ahead for the smoothest user experience possible. Your goal should be to anticipate your visitors' tasks, and then make them as easy to accomplish as possible. What this means in terms of a theme's design will vary on a case-by-case basis, naturally. By studying the types of websites that you think accomplish similar goals to yours, you can figure out ahead what works for the audience.

Planning Milestone

■ What will the ideal site visit using this theme look like? Outline a few tasks that a visitor of your theme might want to accomplish.

Planning for Publishers

Now that you've put some thought into the visitor experience for sites powered by your theme, it's time to consider the direct users of your theme: the publishers. WordPress is primarily a publishing platform. Planning for the authors who will use your theme to publish their content is just as vital—if not more so—to the success of your theme as considering the sites' visitors.

As with your target audience, it's impossible to pinpoint the type of author who's going to be using your theme. Even within a specific group (let's say, casual photographers), there'll be an array of authors with varying levels of experience. For instance, some photographers will be quite comfortable filling out several custom fields in a blog post, having years of experience using their own custom HTML and CSS. Others, however, will be hard-pressed to figure out how to publish a simple post.

As a general rule, you should plan your theme for the least-experienced user—within reason, of course. If you're planning a photography theme, it's safe to assume that most authors will understand to some degree how digital images work (for example, a concept as basic as how a thumbnail image is different from a full-size image). However, it would be best not to take for granted that the average photographer understands how to make a thumbnail image trigger a JavaScript lightbox to reveal a larger image. So if you include this type of functionality, it's important that you make it easy to use, and include clear instructions in your theme package (the topic of instructional material will be covered in greater detail in Chapter 8).

Take time to investigate the features that you think authors using your theme will want. Think about the types of design to which they're likely to be drawn. And, as much as possible, support such brainstorming with research; for instance, ask people you know who fit your target author profile what they'd want in a theme.

Planning Milestone

■ What can you reasonably expect your theme's publishers to know about running a website?
■ Are you planning on including features that might be beyond the reach of the average author?

Planning for Organization and Hierarchy

At this point in the planning process, you should have a fairly good idea of the content your theme will excel at delivering, as well as the design and features that best complement the content. You've also spent time thinking about how to ideally serve the theme's audience and its users. Finally, you've researched the themes, plugins, and scripts currently on the market to refine those design ideas into a more unified vision, preferably with a well-defined feature list.

What this information amounts to is a feature set that will distinguish your theme from any other. Now it's time to figure out how to turn that feature set into an organized wireframe for the design process.

Let's start by laying out a few basic principles of a usable WordPress theme. Regardless of your archetype, these content guidelines will be relevant. Your content should adhere to these principles:

Easy to navigate
> Whether your theme is intended for sprawling, multi-author blogs or small, five-page business sites, the core content has to be easy to find and navigate. Visitors should be able to readily understand how to navigate the site within seconds of arriving. The content on each page should have a clear visual hierarchy, and the site's pages should be linked in a logical organizational structure.

Easy to engage with
> Carefully consider which interactive features you want to include, such as comments, social media share links, and anything else that helps visitors engage with the site's content.

Easy to organize
> Plan for the effective use and display of categories, tags, and search functionality. Visitors should be able to find a particular blog post or page in your theme without having to resort to Google.

Organization is all about how you're going to slice and dice the content. In this phase of the planning, you should return to the breakdown of a WordPress theme's components that we saw in the section called "What do you start with?" and decide how you want to put those pieces together to form a functional site theme. In order to do that, you'll want to start drawing a sitemap that shows how the various pages connect, and wireframes showing what content is presented on each of these pages. Throughout this process, keep the three principles of organization front and center in your mind, and use them (along with your theme's mission statement) to guide you with any decisions.

The Theme Sitemap and Wireframe

Creating sitemaps and wireframes for WordPress themes is a little different from designing them for a standard website because, in a WordPress theme, the final content is unknown. It's impossible to anticipate how many pages, subpages, or blog posts will need to be accommodated, and you'll be unable to plan for the exact content on specific pages or in particular regions of the page. However, you still have to draw out your theme's core content structure and plan ahead for where individual pieces of content will show up on each page. These two tasks are the domain of the sitemap and the wireframe, respectively.

The Sitemap

Most WordPress sitemaps look quite similar, but how you organize the content is what will be unique to your theme. Evidently, you should plan for the variation that individual publishers will bring to your theme. Remember that they'll be able to add any number of posts in any number of categories, not to mention any number of pages and subpages.

Some of the questions you'll need to consider are:

- Will you have blog posts on the home page? Will blog posts be presented in full, with excerpts, or only as a list of titles?

- How will users navigate from the front page to each page or blog post? How will they move between posts?

- Are there any custom features on your list that need to be included in the sitemap? For instance, you might require both a featured post spot as well as a custom category loop on the home page. If a feature affects the way that content is organized, make note of it on the sitemap.

A sitemap is also a great place to start recording which custom page templates you want to include. Some examples might be a custom image-gallery page template, a full-width template (with no sidebar), or another form of specialized content layout.

There is a nearly limitless number of ways that you can approach your theme's sitemap, but let's take a peek at two examples for the sake of highlighting differences, in Figure 2.5 and Figure 2.6.

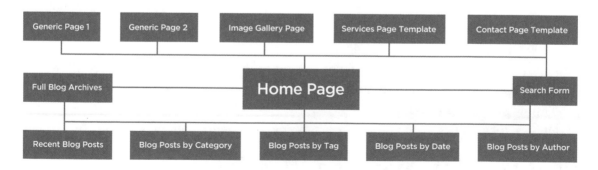

Figure 2.5. An example WordPress sitemap

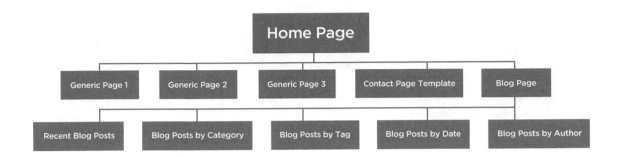

Figure 2.6. An alternative sitemap

In these two sitemap examples, notice how users arrive at the blog content differently. In the sitemap shown in Figure 2.5, the home page serves as a hub for all the blog content. Conversely, in the sitemap in Figure 2.6, all the blog content is tucked away in a blog section, which is reached by clicking a link on the home page. What you do with your own sitemap will ultimately depend on how you want to guide users through your theme.

The Wireframe

When building wireframes for a WordPress theme, you need to sketch out the sections of the layout that are reserved for particular kinds of content. This will directly influence the first step in your design phase, so be as accurate as possible. You can be as advanced as you want, but in my experience you need at least four wireframes worked out before you can begin designing, to be used for:

- the home page
- a default page view
- a single post view
- lists of posts (for example, archive pages, search results, or category or tag pages)

In each of these four core wireframes—shown in Figure 2.7 through to Figure 2.10—take note that the core layout barely changes. Generally, the only aspect changing from one wireframe to the next is the structure of the content inside the main column.

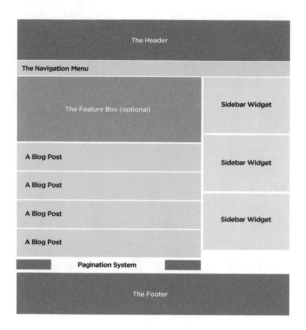

Figure 2.7. A home page wireframe

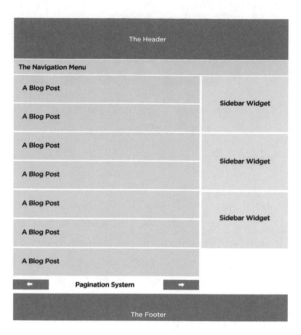

Figure 2.8. A post list page wireframe

Figure 2.9. A single-post page wireframe

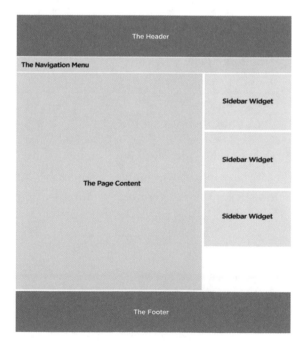

Figure 2.10. A WordPress page wireframe

You can also create wireframes for each custom page template you want to include, in addition to layout sketches for any custom features (such as lightboxes or galleries) that you might need once you enter the design phase.

Let's take a look at a couple of different home page wireframes for the purpose of illustrating just how simple a wireframe can be (as well as how different two unique wireframes can look). We'll look at one wireframe for a text-heavy blog in Figure 2.11, and another for a photo blog in Figure 2.12.

Notice that, while both wireframes are quite simple, each illustrates a unique layout that addresses the type of content that each blog will focus on. We'll be concentrating on the design phase of the theme creation process in the next chapter, so at this point your wireframes can be as simple and straightforward as you'd like. If it feels like something is missing at this point, don't fret: we'll be digging into the nitty gritty details of what makes up a WordPress theme next!

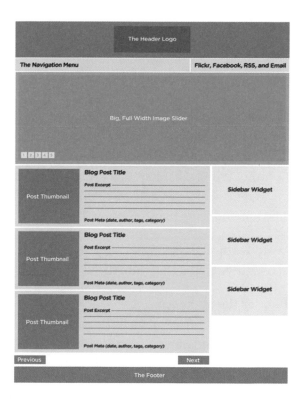

Figure 2.11. A home page wireframe for a text-heavy theme   Figure 2.12. A home page wireframe for a photo-based theme

Just Recapping ...

Planning your theme using this process is a valuable way to clarify its major elements before starting the design phase. There's no need for planning to be especially lengthy, or even organized in any formal way—a notepad, text editor, or napkin will do just fine—but you should at least jot down your plans. This is particularly true if it's one of your first custom themes. To be frank, some people's planning is limited to brainstorming on the treadmill at the gym. Personally, I still make extensive notes after having created 100 themes, but in the end you should use whatever workflow makes you feel most comfortable.

Regardless of which method you select, you should establish the following before you start the design process:

- your theme's main goal
- the type(s) of content that your theme will focus on
- a list of features that you would like to include in your theme
- knowledge of the sort of publishers and audience that will use your theme
- a strategy for how your theme will handle blog posts, pages, categories, tags, and custom fields
- an idea of what content will be displayed on each of the theme's main page types

Before we move on to the design phase, let's review some ideas to ponder throughout the planning process:

Define success

What is the mission statement for your theme?

Let your content lead the way

What is the primary content type going to be for your theme? Will you be including a mix of other types of content that need to planned for? What are the key features that must be included to deliver the theme's core content? How will your site's general layout support that content? Will you have two columns? Three columns? Try to be as specific as possible.

Avoid feature bloat

Without detracting from its primary goal, what additional features should your theme include?

Plan for the audience

What will the ideal visitor's path through this theme look like? Outline a few quick tasks that a visitor of your theme might want to accomplish, and plan ahead for making those tasks as easy to accomplish as possible.

Plan for the publishers

What can you reasonably expect your target authors to know? Are you planning on including features that might be so hard to use that they will confuse the average author? Are there any features authors will want that you've neglected?

Do some research

Scout out the Internet for new ideas. Make a list of the scripts, plugins, and themes that you like; then go back to your previous feature list and revise it as needed.

Plan for organization and hierarchy

How do you plan to organize the content inside your WordPress theme? Where will pages go within the layout? How will blog posts be treated? Will you have any specialized category or tag loops anywhere? What other custom organization or hierarchy notes should you make?

The theme sitemap and wireframe

Create a theme sitemap and a few wireframes that you can reference during the design process.

If you have answers to all these questions, congratulations! You're well on your way to developing a great WordPress theme. Don't pull out your code editor just yet, though: there's still more design work to be done. In the next chapter, we'll be taking the guidelines we developed in this chapter and turning them into a fully fleshed-out design.

Theme Design 101

by Brandon R. Jones

With your theme planned out and a set of rough wireframes in hand, it's time to start the design phase. This is my favorite part of the entire process, because it's where you make your vision come to life! The goal of the design phase is to end up with a fully realized set of mockups for your theme to use as a basis for the development phase.

This chapter will be broken up into two main sections: first, we'll review how the traditional principles of good web design specifically relate to WordPress; then, we'll discuss the anatomy of a WordPress theme, with examples of how you can approach the design of each component of your theme.

 The Tools of the Trade

Before you start designing, you'll want to decide on a favorite method of mocking up your ideas. Many designers (myself included) use Adobe Photoshop as their software of choice, but I would be remiss to suggest that this is the only tool out there. In addition to using quite a few other competent graphic-creation applications, you can also theoretically do all of your designing directly by coding the CSS on the fly (which some ultra-fast coders prefer). I've even seen designers mock up everything by hand.

Whatever method you pick is fine, but it's worth noting that there are some key advantages to using Photoshop (or a similar program) to design your theme:

■ It's the industry norm. You'll end up with an industry-standard file that you can give to people using your theme, which makes it easier for them to implement changes.

■ It's more organized. You'll be able to quickly organize your image layers into folders. I personally use a different folder in my Photoshop files for each page template in my theme, so that I can quickly toggle the page design I am working on.

■ It makes redesigning a breeze. Creating a new skin of the theme will be as easy as creating some duplicate layers and customizing them.

The Principles of WordPress Theme Design

The following section is intended to be a quick primer on how core design principles will play into a WordPress theme. It's worth mentioning that there are some terrific books that discuss these principles in a lot more detail than I'll go into here. *Sexy Web Design*[1] and *The Principles of Beautiful Web Design*[2] are two excellent starting points from SitePoint. If you're new to the design process, I'd highly recommend digging in a little deeper to familiarize yourself with the principles of design. With that said, this section should serve as a solid review for readers of all levels of experience.

 Plan for Customization

Unless you're designing a WordPress theme for a single-use website, it's always a good strategy to design with customization in mind. Most of the publishers using your site will want to make it their own, either by adding their logo and adjusting a few colors, or by rearranging the sidebar and menus, for example.

Although coding is reserved for a later chapter, it's still important to consider at this stage which portions of your theme design will be constant (the layout, content structure, and so on) and which portions will be variable (colors, fonts, and the like). You can make your theme more skinnable by separating the core, unchanging elements from the superficial, variable ones. If the publisher wants to make a change, they won't need to go digging in your theme's core; they'll just need to swap one skin file for another. Or, better yet, you can make the skin selection a custom option in your theme's administration section (Allan will be covering this in Chapter 7). Even if you're designing a theme for a single site, this separation practice is still a good idea: it will make changes down the road much easier.

Color

Entire books have been written about color theory, so I'll avoid going into too much detail here. It's assumed that you'll select a harmonious color scheme that works with your vision for the theme. What matters in a theme design is not about the kind of color scheme you use, but rather *how* you implement it in your theme.

---

[1] http://www.sitepoint.com/books/sexy1/
[2] http://www.sitepoint.com/books/design1/

Color has an important function in terms of branding any website. If color plays a dominant role in the theme (for example, if the site's background is a vibrant red), publishers will likely want to have control over that color to suit their own brand colors. Figure 3.1 shows an example of a template design that allows for customization of the color without any change to the core layout.

Figure 3.1. The Iconic Theme comes in a variety of color options

Notice how the custom color is used in a number of places in the theme: the background color of the header and footer, the large buttons at the top of the front page, and the standard link color.

In addition to considering how color is utilized for the important elements of the page, you can also make your theme "pop" just by changing the color of decorative elements: using horizontal color stripes, bullets, frames for images, colorful sidebar elements, and bold splashes of color in the footer, for instance.

There's more to color than being decorative, though. Figure 3.2 and Figure 3.3 are examples of themes in which color takes a more central role in the overall feel of the design.

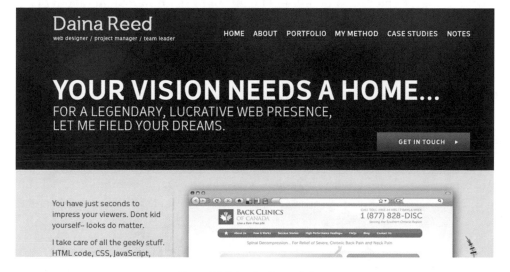

Figure 3.2. Daina Reed's purple hues

Figure 3.3. The BountyBev site embraces the color blue

Branding

If you're designing a theme that will be used by a wide range of publishers, it's important that you consider the role brand will play.

Logos come in a wide range of sizes, colors, and formats. Make sure that your design allows for publishers to use their own logo (or add text for their site title when they don't have an image). This may seem like obvious advice, but the consideration here is that the theme's logo space should allow for a variety of possibilities.

Many site owners want to include a prominent tagline or mission statement (about one to two sentences long) for the blog or company that's prominent on the front page. Make sure you plan for this when building your design.

Additionally, you may want to consider different font stacks to allow publishers to change the tone of their site by selecting an alternative typeface.

Typography

Because WordPress sites often use a lot of text, you should be devoting some serious thought to your theme's typography. While there are probably tens of thousands of unique visual combinations achievable through CSS font styling, there are a few main points that you should consider.

Uniformity

Regardless of the font style you pick, it's important that you be constant in your font treatment throughout your theme. Using several fonts can make your theme look disorganized and unprofessional. It can also serve to confuse publishers about which fonts to use in which contexts. The best typographic systems use one or two typefaces to develop sophisticated and readable blocks of text on every page.

Hierarchy

Use the size and styling of your type to develop the hierarchy on each of your theme's templates. Traditional print design is an ideal place from which to draw inspiration. Consider a newspaper: the front page will boldly display the main headlines, the lesser articles will receive smaller, but still legible headlines, and the body copy will always be small and uniform from article to article.

Like the majority of newspaper publishers worldwide, the *New York Times* has carried over the typographic hierarchy from the print publication to its website, as shown in Figure 3.4. Notice that there are three story headline font sizes: one for the feature story, another for the secondary story in the first editorial column and the photo highlight, and a third for all the other abstracts on the front page.

Also, look at how typography is used to establish a hierarchy in the section listing in the far left menu: you can tell at a glance that "Books" and "Movies" are subsections of "Arts."

Figure 3.4. Typographic hierarchy on *The New York Times* website

Let's carry this metaphor over to your WordPress theme. The home page template of your theme should promptly let users know where they are and what the site's primary content is. Post and page titles should be easy to find, read, and click on. Subheadings should be less dominant and so forth, until you have styled the body copy, which should be simple, readable, and consistent across all parts of the site.

You can of course use other visual design elements to organize content on your pages, but be mindful of the power that type has to communicate information hierarchy. In WordPress themes especially, it's a powerful way to ensure that content is communicated clearly—even if you're unsure what that content is going to be.

Line Length, Letter Spacing, and Line Height

These elements of design are often overlooked, as the browser defaults are generally seen as being "good enough." But paying close attention to how these small details will complement your theme's layout and visual style is often the difference between a good design and one that is truly awesome.

Text should have plenty of room to breathe, and lines of text should avoid being so long that it's difficult for the eye to scan back to the beginning of the next line. This second point is particularly relevant to flexible-width layouts: consider how the text will stretch if the site is being viewed on a very wide monitor.

Font Replacement

Typography on the Web has recently been undergoing a form of renaissance. Previously designers were limited to relying on a user's installed fonts for CSS styling, or replacing the text with an image or (shudder) Flash movie; now, a number of new font replacement and embedding technologies have become available, allowing you use of virtually any font, so long as the license terms allow it.

You should abstain from using font replacement for body text; instead, limit it to headings, titles, blockquotes, and the like. A custom font can give your theme a distinct personality. Here are few other rules of thumb (break them at your own risk):

- Avoid using fonts that are hard to read.

- Don't use more than one font face as a font replacement unless you have a very good reason.

- Make sure that browsers will still render legible type when the font replacement doesn't occur. This means paying attention to line height, font color, and letter spacing. The same rules discussed in the main typography section apply to font replacement.

- Consider the implications of using a specific typeface on non-English language sites. If your theme is likely to be used with a language that requires characters missing from that typeface, you need to plan for a fallback or alternative font.

Let's look at a few sites that make clever use of font replacement. Figure 3.5 is a great example: the two distinct header fonts complement each other nicely and contribute to the visual style of the site.

Figure 3.5. Complementary font replacement on The Sew Weekly

The site shown in Figure 3.6 also uses a few well-chosen custom fonts to contribute to the feel and style of the design.

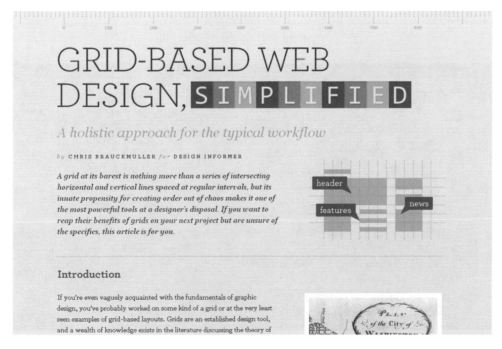

Figure 3.6. Custom fonts on Design Informer, simplified

Visual Style

Color, typography, and texture combine to create a unique visual style for your theme. By having a clear idea from the outset of what you're trying to achieve, you'll be better able to combine the distinct parts into a cohesive whole.

Think about the tone and context that you are trying to achieve when arriving at a visual style. Figure 3.7 and Figure 3.8 illustrate two individual visual styles. Consider the message that each style conveys without reading any of the words on the pages.

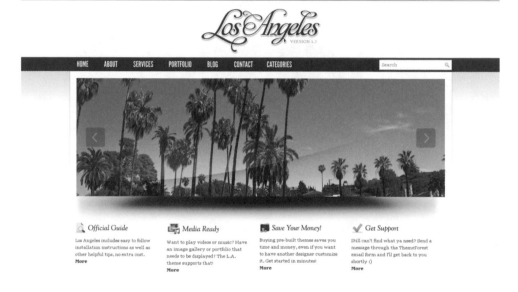

Figure 3.7. The Los Angeles Theme

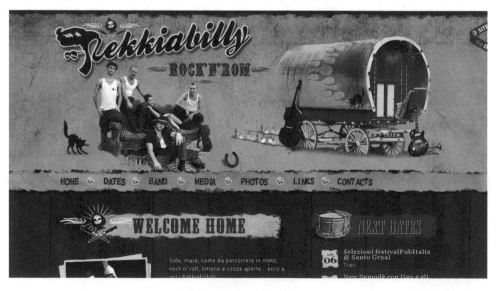

Figure 3.8. www.rekkiabilly.com

As seen here, the visual style of your theme can range from clean and minimal to bold and illustrative (and everything in between). If you're designing a theme that a range of people will use, you should limit the visual styling to simple, unobtrusive elements, as these are much easier to customize. Conversely, if you're designing a theme for a specific niche, you'll have a lot more room to maneuver.

Layout and Composition

At the end of Chapter 2, I discussed the importance of drawing wireframes that map out the content contained on each page of your theme, and how that content will be organized. Now that we've reached the design phase, it's time to map out the theme's layout in more detail. Selecting the layout of your theme is one of the most crucial decisions to make during the design process.

The Golden Ratio

Dating back to the Renaissance art period, the **golden ratio** is simply a mathematical ratio that's widespread in nature, and which tends to give compositions an aesthetically pleasing balance. Everything from an oil painting to a web design can use the ratio. The ratio is fairly close to (but not exactly) a two-thirds to one-third split, as illustrated in Figure 3.9.

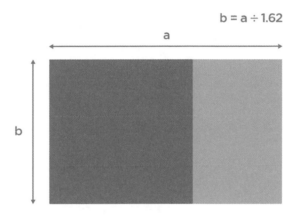

Figure 3.9. The golden ratio

In a WordPress theme, the golden ratio usually appears as the ratio of the main content column to the sidebar column; it can also be applied to subcolumns, or to the height of elements in the header or footer. Let's look at a practical example of what this might mean for your theme layout. A typical site layout is shown in Figure 3.10.

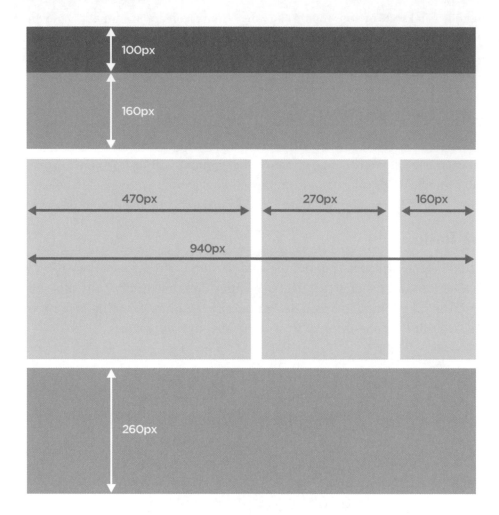

Figure 3.10. The golden ratio applied to a site layout

This wireframe actually uses the golden ratio to guide its column and row proportions. The 470px column is balanced against the 270px column, which in turn is balanced against the 160px column. In the header, the two sections are also proportionate to the golden ratio. Notice how pleasing this layout is to the eye. Every column and row works in harmony with the other elements in the template to create a balanced, yet interesting, visual structure.

Fixed or Fluid

Because web pages are viewed on a number of screen sizes and resolutions, it's worth considering how the theme will adapt to all of the various options. Most desktop screen sizes are above 1000px wide by 600px tall (after you remove the browser and operating system chrome). Mobile browsers naturally have a lot less screen real estate to work with, though some—like the iPhone—compensate by zooming the entire page out to fit on the screen.

Your theme can have a fluid width—that is, it can adapt itself to the size of the browser window—or it can be a fixed width. There are pros and cons associated with either approach, though fixed-width designs seem to be increasing in popularity as ultra-wide monitors become more prevalent. They're also a little easier to code: no more worrying about your layout breaking at a given window size.

But, as with all design decisions associated with your theme, the layout you pick will depend on your theme's goals and mission statement.

Layout Options

After considering your layout in the abstract, you'll need to select the dimensions for your theme. In most cases a maximum width of 960px is advisable, because it will display on the majority of screen sizes: your theme will be viewable on a monitor with a resolution of 1024x768px, without any nasty horizontal scrollbars. Even if you've chosen to build a theme with a fluid width, you should still start the design phase with a set of dimensions in mind, so that you can establish the default proportions of various elements.

There are a few traditional options from which to pick when considering your layout. The most common ones around are your garden variety two-column and three-column layouts, which adapt well to a number of uses; for simple sites, though, a single-column layout can be effective. Examples of these layouts (in numerical order) are shown in Figure 3.11, Figure 3.12, and Figure 3.13.

Figure 3.11. A single-column layout

Figure 3.12. A two-column layout

Figure 3.13. A three-column layout

These conventional layouts are attractive and functional to boot. However, there's no need to be limited by convention! There's a host of newer WordPress themes that are truly outside of most people's perceptions of a WordPress theme. Figure 3.14 and Figure 3.15 are examples of WordPress themes that use original and unconventional layouts.

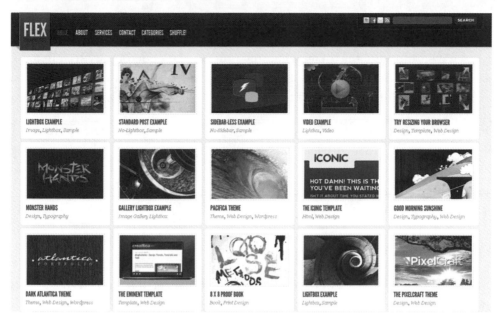

Figure 3.14. The Flex Theme utilizes a flexible grid layout

Figure 3.15. Brizk Design's website uses a fixed navigation and a vertically scrolling main body section

Keeping customization in mind, you might also want to plan for multiple layouts and allow your users to pick the one they prefer. You could also provide a few custom page layouts that your users can apply to specific pages on their sites (this will be discussed further in Chapter 7).

The Anatomy of a WordPress Theme

In Chapter 2, we went through the theme planning process and ended up with a sitemap and a few wireframes. Now, with the help of the design principles we've seen in this chapter so far, we'll be turning your wireframes into the actual bits and pieces from which a WordPress theme is made.

But just what are those bits and pieces? Like many other content management platforms, WordPress treats most pages and posts in a very modular way. This means that the sidebar on one page will almost always look like the sidebar on another page. The same goes for the header, footer, and other elements. There are several of these modules that come together to form a complete WordPress theme, and it's important that you understand and address each one in the design phase. In addition, there are a number of specific pages that just about every site will need, and these should be part of your theme: 404 error pages and search results pages, for example.

If you leave one or more of these components undesigned, you will be forced to come up with an appearance for them on the fly when you start coding your CSS; this can often lead to those elements having a poorly defined visual style, or seeming at odds with the rest of your design. By addressing every component in the design phase, you'll ensure that your theme will have a consistent feel that's slick and professional.

A few of the core components of a standard WordPress home page template are shown in Figure 3.16.

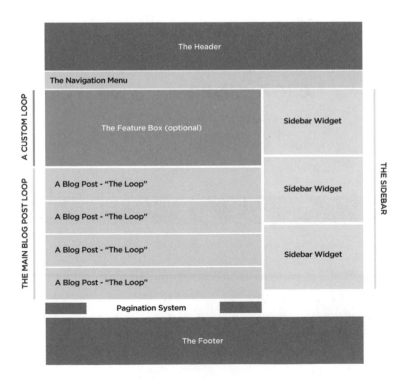

Figure 3.16. The anatomy of a WordPress home page

We'll now examine each component in turn, and I'll show you some fine examples of design that should inspire you with ideas about how to implement them in your theme. After that, we'll address the design of each of the page types in our sitemap. By the end of this section, your head will be spinning with ideas, and you should be raring to start on your own theme's design.

The Header

First impressions matter. Being the first element visitors see when they reach a site, the header is crucial to establishing the site's tone and message. A clean, uncluttered header is a safe way to go, but it's far from being the only one, as we'll shortly see.

The header will almost always include the site's branding, logo, and possibly its mission statement. Depending on your site's layout, the header might also include a navigation menu, a search bar, or other elements like links for RSS feeds, social media, login and registration, as well as banner ad spots.

Figure 3.17 through to Figure 3.23 show how versatile a site header can be.

Figure 3.17. This header includes the site navigation, login functionality, and a bold mission statement

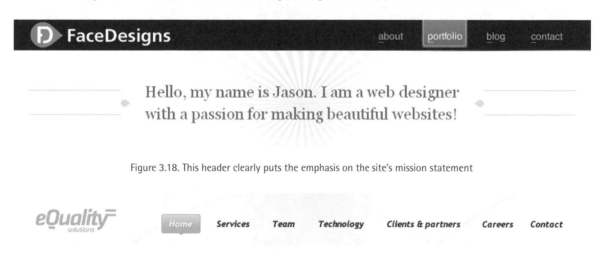

Figure 3.18. This header clearly puts the emphasis on the site's mission statement

Figure 3.19. A minimal header containing only navigation and branding is suitable for the widest range of sites

Figure 3.20. A much larger header that includes a mission statement and feature carousel

Figure 3.21. An example of a more goal-centered header with a couple of clear calls to action

Figure 3.22. This header uses color and branding elements to establish the site's personality

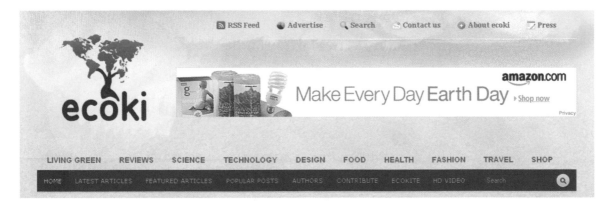

Figure 3.23. A more involved header with multilevel navigation and a banner ad spot

Take a moment to note what sets each header apart from the next in these examples. Is the header's goal simply to set the design tone and feel for the site? To convey the site's mission statement? Or is it to encourage the user to do a specific task, like request a quote or share the site with their friends?

The trick is to use the header to highlight content that's important to your own theme goals. Make sure that it works in harmony with your overall mission statement for the rest of the theme. Remember, it's your job as a designer to help guide users to the most relevant content. A successful header immediately tells users where they are and what kind of content they'll find at the site; it should also make it simple to find the most important content. If your header design accomplishes those goals, the rest is just icing on the cake.

The Navigation Menu

All the previous headers shown in this chapter included the site's main navigation. As navigation is such a necessary part of a site, let's spend some time focusing on navigation menus in particular. Traditionally they appear at the top of the page—horizontally—but your theme can incorporate any number of navigation displays, from a vertically listed sidebar to a fancy menu that reveals itself when the mouse hovers over it. Keep in mind that as well as the top-level links, you'll also need to design for the subpages and sub-subpages. Drop-down menus are often a perfect solution for these nested hierarchies; a few examples are shown in Figure 3.24 and Figure 3.25.

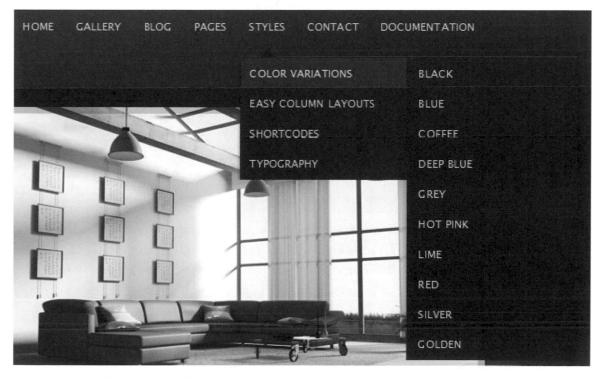

Figure 3.24. The InFocus theme includes jQuery-animated drop-down menus for all subpages

Figure 3.25. A similar drop-down menu on the CleanCut theme

A navigation menu can also include extras like categories (as shown in Figure 3.26), the blogroll, or any other links that you think will be useful to visitors. While it's important that you avoid having your site's main menu cluttered with too many options, there's no need to limit yourself to just pages.

Figure 3.26. The Los Angeles theme includes a navigation menu item for categories

How you treat the visual styling of the navigation is also a significant consideration. Often, visual cues serve to help orientate users by making it obvious which page they're currently on. A clear example, where tabs are used for this purpose, is shown in Figure 3.27. Even if tabs or buttons are unsuited to your theme's style or layout, it's important to ensure that your navigation is easy to find, read, and use.

Figure 3.27. delibarapp.com uses tabs to give the site's navigation a physical feel

The Loop

This is arguably the most vital piece of your entire WordPress theme. The Loop is the element that WordPress uses to display posts, whether on the home page, list pages, or single post pages. The Loop will generally include the title of the post, its content (or an excerpt of it), and some metadata such as tags, categories, the author name, and the date of the post.

Figure 3.28 shows the way The Loop is styled in WordPress 3.0's default theme, Twenty Ten. It's quite basic, but all the elements are there, so it's a good starting point for your design.

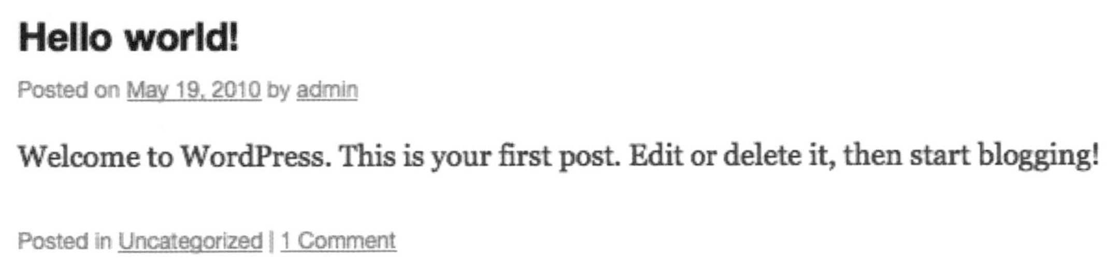

Hello world!

Posted on May 19, 2010 by admin

Welcome to WordPress. This is your first post. Edit or delete it, then start blogging!

Posted in Uncategorized | 1 Comment

Figure 3.28. The Loop from the home page in the Twenty Ten theme

In a plain old vanilla theme, all posts in The Loop will look the same. But life isn't plain old vanilla, and nor does your WordPress Loop need to be. You can create custom designs for The Loop for various types of content; for example, one layout for a text post and another for a video post, or perhaps different styles for each category.

When considering your own design for The Loop, return to your mission statement and decide what pieces of content are pertinent to your theme's success. If you're designing an image blog, you might opt to show a thumbnail and a title with a few tags. Alternatively, if you're designing The Loop for a theme comprising mainly text content, additional metadata such as the post's date, author, categories, and tags can be helpful for users seeking content relevant to their interests. The examples in Figure 3.29 through to Figure 3.30 show what you can do with The Loop.

11.09.2008 | Grandchild Category I | 9 Comments

A Post With Everything In It

Lorem ipsum dolor sit amet, consectetuer adipiscing elit. Curabitur quam augue, vehicula quis, tincidunt vel, varius vitae, nulla. Sed convallis orci. Duis libero orci, pretium a, _convallis quis_, pellentesque a, dolor. Curabitur vitae nisi non dolor vestibulum consequat.

 read more

Figure 3.29. The Loop with a post thumbnail

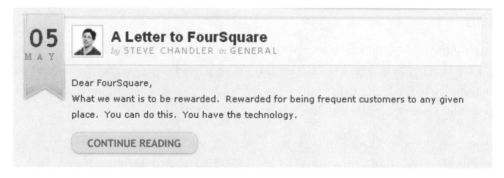

Figure 3.30. A prominent date and **Continue Reading** button are more pragmatic features

Widgets on iPhone OS 4.0

23. FEB, 2010

Dimitri Stancioff questions the lack of utility apps (Weather, Stocks, etc.) in the_iPad demos_ and raises the possibility of a secret "Dashboard" app.

LEAVE A COMMENT

0 Comments

Tweet This

Short URL

Figure 3.31. To facilitate sharing, here The Loop includes Tweet This and Short URL links

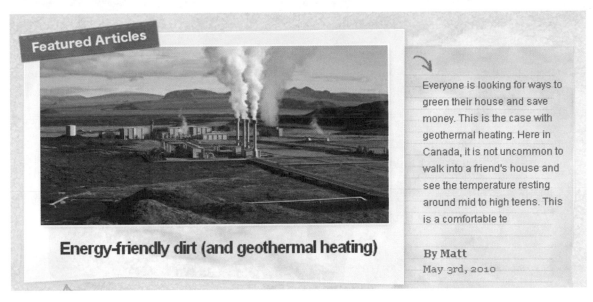

Figure 3.32. Further design possibilities include large feature images and textured backgrounds

Pagination

Wherever posts are listed, WordPress will automatically split the list into pages if there are more than a set amount. The pagination controls are the links that allow users to navigate back and forth through these list pages. The pagination control is usually placed at the bottom of the page, after The Loop, but often it might feature at both the top and bottom. It can be made up of Next and Previous links, as in Figure 3.33, or a numbered list of pages, as in Figure 3.34.

Figure 3.33. A simple Next/Previous pagination control

Figure 3.34. A more complex pagination system

These examples highlight that you need to consider more than just the appearance of the pagination controls: you also need to think about how they'll work. The standard Next/Previous links work well for simple sites and keep the design tidy, but when you have a large amount of content, it's advisable to give users a more direct way to find older content, rather than hitting the **Previous** button 20 times in a row.

Comments

WordPress's comment system is a big draw for publishers, so you should definitely pay attention to this part of your theme! For many sites it will be the primary point of engagement between the site and its readers, so it's worth spending a little extra time designing it.

There are two components to the comment system that need to be addressed in a theme. The first is the form that visitors will use to post comments, featuring the name, email address, website URL, and, of course, comment text fields.

The examples inFigure 3.35 to Figure 3.38 show approaches to the form's design, ranging from the extremely simple to the more complex.

Figure 3.35. A simple and clearly laid-out comment form

Figure 3.36. Now for a more personal feel

Figure 3.37. Note this form's email notification checkbox and required fields

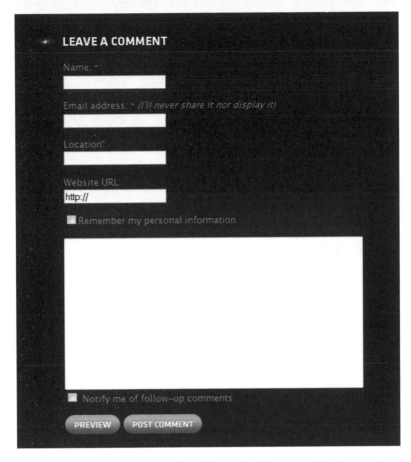

Figure 3.38. Here users are able to preview their posts in advance, as well as be remembered

As the latter examples prove, there are certainly a few bells and whistles at your disposal to spruce up the plain old comment form. You need to be aware that publishers using your theme may want to employ these features, and plan for them in the design phase. The Subscribe to Comments plugin,[3] which adds the **Notify me of follow-up comments** checkbox seen in Figure 3.37 and Figure 3.38 above, is one highly popular example. There are also a number of plugins that provide comment preview functionality, so it's worth incorporating this handy feature as well.

The second major component of WordPress's comment system is, of course, the comments themselves. Each comment should show the name of the poster—usually as a link back to the website URL they've provided—as well as the date the comment was posted and the actual comment text. WordPress makes use of the Gravatar[4] author thumbnail service by default, so you should plan for displaying avatars with the comments.

---

[3] http://wordpress.org/extend/plugins/subscribe-to-comments/
[4] http://cn.gravatar.com/

Threaded Comments

Threaded commenting, a relatively new feature to WordPress, allows visitors to reply to previous comments. As a result, the replies will often be displayed indented under the "parent" comment, rather than in an aligned chronological list. It's highly advisable that your theme at least *support* threaded commenting; individual publishers may select to opt out of this feature, but as it's standard in WordPress, you'll need to ensure that it works for publishers who do choose to allow it.

Let's take a look at some well-designed comment lists in Figure 3.39, Figure 3.40, and Figure 3.41. You'll notice the clear separation between comments, as well as author thumbnails and prominent reply buttons.

5 RESPONSES AND COUNTING...

admin
10.12.2009
Edit

Vivamus nibh mi, commodo eu, pellentesque ut, blandit rutrum, ligula. Praesent ultricies urna a urna. Quisque massa. Cras ipsum diam, hendrerit id, accumsan sit amet, fermentum vel, dui. Morbi blandit commodo tellus. Aenean tincidunt pharetra leo. Curabitur euismod sollicitudin elit. Donec faucibus lacus nec sapien. Aliquam ipsum nisi, scelerisque et, commodo nec, consectetur vel, tellus. Cras ipsum diam, hendrerit id, accumsan sit amet, fermentum vel, dui. Morbi blandit commodo tellus.

admin
Edit

Lorem ipsum dolor sit amet, consectetur adipiscing elit. Vivamus nibh mi, commodo eu, pellentesque ut, blandit rutrum, ligula. Praesent ultricies urna a urna. Quisque massa. Cras ipsum diam, hendrerit id, accumsan sit amet, fermentum vel, dui. Morbi blandit commodo tellus. Aenean tincidunt pharetra leo. Curabitur euismod sollicitudin elit. Donec faucibus lacus nec sapien. Aliquam ipsum nisi, scelerisque et, commodo nec, consectetur vel, tellus. Cras ipsum diam, hendrerit id, accumsan sit amet, fermentum vel, dui. Morbi blandit commodo tellus.

Reid
Edit

Aenean tincidunt pharetra leo. Curabitur euismod sollicitudin elit. Donec faucibus lacus nec sapien. Aliquam ipsum nisi, scelerisque et, commodo nec, consectetur vel, tellus. Cras ipsum diam, hendrerit id, accumsan sit amet, fermentum vel, dui. Morbi blandit commodo tellus. Curabitur euismod sollicitudin elit. Donec faucibus lacus nec sapien. Aliquam ipsum nisi, scelerisque et, commodo nec, consectetur vel, tellus. Cras ipsum diam, hendrerit id, accumsan sit amet, fermentum vel, dui. Morbi blandit commodo tellus.

Shane
Pearlman
Edit

This is an example of a WordPress comment, you could edit this to put information about yourself or your site so readers know where you are coming from. You can create as many pages like this one or sub-pages as you like and manage all of your content inside of WordPress. Lorem ipsum dolor sit amet, consectetur adipiscing elit. Nulla neque ipsum, rhoncus eu euismod sed, ullamcorper a urna.

Aiden
Edit

Nice theme!

Figure 3.39. Clear and legible comment design

Figure 3.40. This comment list features alternating background colors between posts and big **Reply** buttons

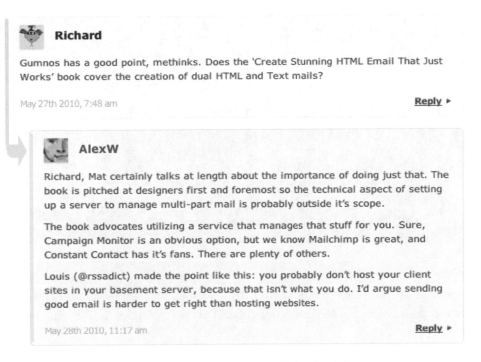

Figure 3.41. The SitePoint blogs use an arrow to display threaded comments

Often comments by the author of the post that's being commented on are styled differently from other comments, in order to stand out, as seen in the last example. This is a common enough feature that many publishers seek out, so it's well worth investigating for inclusion in your theme.

Sidebars and Widgets

The term **sidebar** has a special meaning in WordPress: rather than referring specifically to a column on one side of a page, the sidebar is actually just a section in your layout that can contain user-specified widgets. The sidebar is an incredibly flexible area, so it's worth spending time on the design. The overall appearance should be consistent with the rest of your layout, but the individual widgets can be more accentuated than they are in WordPress's default treatment.

First, just to ground your understanding of what goes into a WordPress sidebar, let's look at the most basic version of the sidebar, highlighted in Figure 3.42.

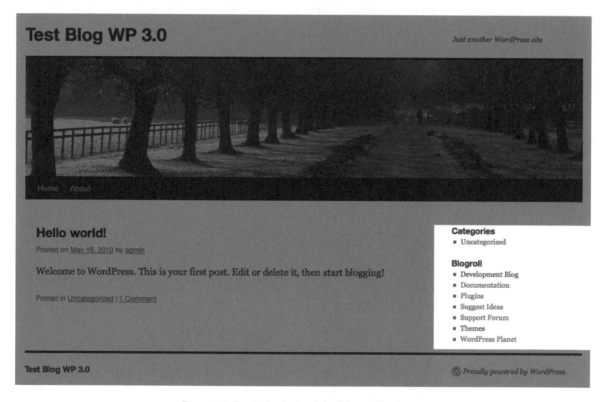

Figure 3.42. The sidebar in the default Twenty Ten theme

Notice that the sidebar includes two elements: widget titles and widget content. Remember those two basic elements as we take a look at other sidebar styles in Figure 3.43 to Figure 3.48.

Figure 3.43. A bookmark-style sidebar

Figure 3.44. A sidebar styled to represent an envelope

Figure 3.45. A clean, minimal sidebar design

Figure 3.46. Some cleverly designed custom widgets in a sidebar

Figure 3.47. Making good use of typography

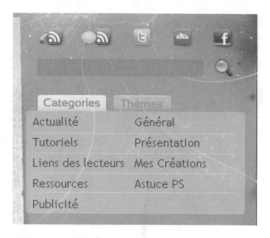

Figure 3.48. Sidebar widgets appear to float above the site's background

Now that we've seen a few creative examples, let's take some time to dissect the sidebar. First of all, a sidebar should be no less than 160 pixels wide to account for the array of widgets out there. Any narrower than that and you risk cramming in too much content for it to be readable, or even breaking the layout of some widgets. Some sidebars can be as large as 300 pixels or more, which is useful if you need to fit standard ad units, such as the popular 300x250px advertisement. Keep in mind that the more space you give to the sidebar, the less you'll have for the content.

Sidebars that Aren't Left on the Side

Remember, a sidebar is just a space that can hold a widget. With a little code wrangling, you can easily have these widget-ready areas in the footer, the header, or even in the middle of The Loop. Just remember the rules: make it a minimum of 160 pixels, style the widget titles, and prepare default styles for the widget content.

WordPress provides about 20 default widgets, but there is a nearly limitless number of plugin widgets out there—from page lists and calendars to social media links and contact forms. You can even include your own custom widgets in your theme (Allan will be showing you how to do this in Chapter 6).

It's impossible to provide a custom design for each widget out there, but the core sidebar elements will always remain the same. If you address the basic elements of font size, padding, margins, widget titles, and widget dividers, chances are you'll end up with a successful sidebar that can hold all manner of widgets that a publisher might want to use. That said, it's still worth testing your theme with as many widgets as you can to see how they look.

The Footer

As the name suggests, the footer of a WordPress theme shows up at the bottom of each page, after the content. For some sites, a conventional colored bar with copyright information and a few links may be appropriate, but this is just a fraction of what can be achieved with a footer; it can provide visitors with some unique content or offer other ways of navigating the site. The footer is like a surprise treat for users who've made it all the way to the bottom of the page, rewarding their interest in the site. If they've made it this far, why not provide them with some fun and useful links?

Let's start by checking out footers that lean towards the simple and conventional style. Figure 3.49, Figure 3.51, and Figure 3.50 are all drawn from the popular theme site WooThemes.com.[5]

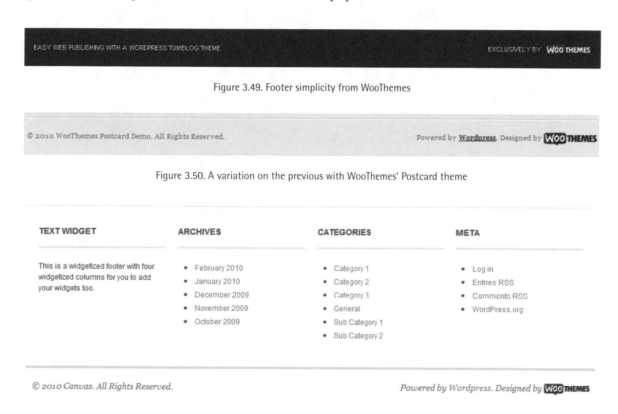

Figure 3.49. Footer simplicity from WooThemes

Figure 3.50. A variation on the previous with WooThemes' Postcard theme

Figure 3.51. WooThemes' Canvas theme footer steps it up a little

These footers display copyright information, a reminder of the site brand, and one has a widget area. They're simple and understated, in keeping with the visual styles of the themes from which they're drawn.

Now to the other end of the spectrum, where we'll see some more extravagant examples of footer designs in Figure 3.52 through to Figure 3.56.

---

[5] http://woothemes.com/

Figure 3.52. This inspired footer design provides additional ways for visitors to interact with the site

Figure 3.53. Oval Cube's footer offers links to posts, news, and Twitter updates

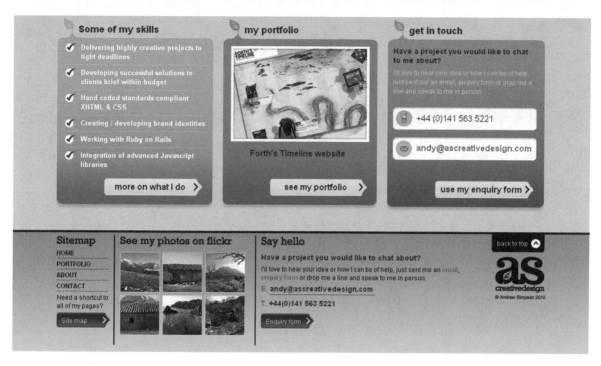

Figure 3.54. This expansive footer presents an array of additional content and contact information

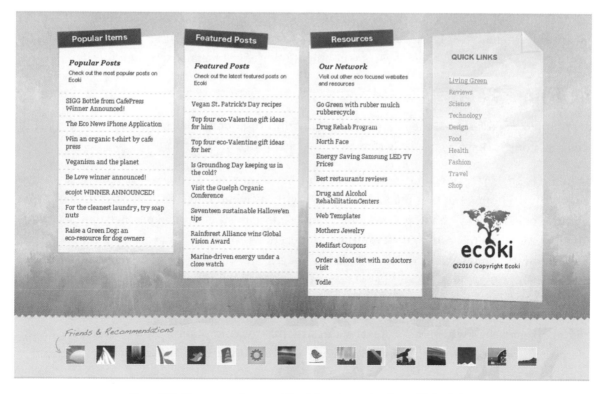

Figure 3.55. Numerous options greet the visitor who reaches the ecoki site footer

Figure 3.56. Sawyer Hollenshead's site footer combines widgets and links for the interested user

The more advanced footers just featured, as well as being highly creative, offer features that complement the site content. These features can serve to redirect users to other content or interaction tools that are of interest to them—users who might otherwise be ready to leave the site.

The Home Page

Now that we've covered all the components of a WordPress theme page, it's time to look at all the pages that constitute a theme. Let's start from the beginning, shall we?

The home page, front page, landing page, splash page—call it what you like, it's the page that your theme will call home, the first place that visitors will see when they arrive at your theme through the front door. The way you approach the front page design is tied to the message that you want to deliver. Show off your best features up front, and users will know right away why they want to stick around. If your theme is going to focus on images, showcase them. If your theme is going to concentrate on video, include a video player on the front page. If you plan to dish out text-heavy content, make your page easy to scan.

The front page design will also set the tone and structure for your other templates, so close attention to detail here will pay off, as Figure 3.57, Figure 3.58, and Figure 3.59 attest.

Figure 3.57. Striking, bold images greet the visitor to the Unite theme's home page

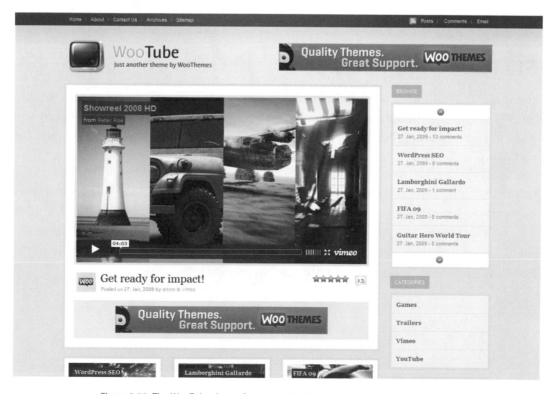

Figure 3.58. The WooTube theme features a sizeable video player on the front page

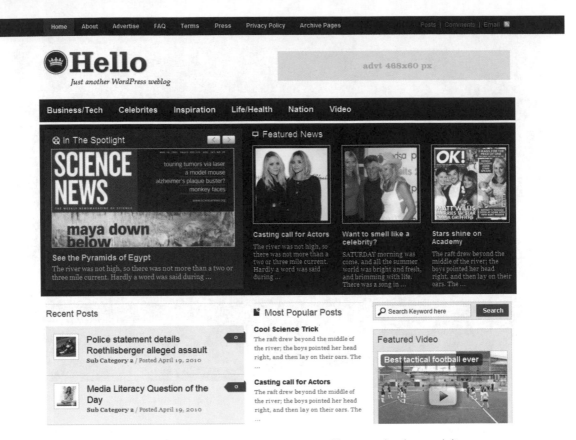

Figure 3.59. The Hello theme home page presents more like a magazine than a website

The Standard Page Template

The standard or default page template is the layout that's used for the theme's page content, such as an About page. Most themes treat the default page template conservatively, since the content itself is fairly static and any special styling might be distracting. The traditional page template includes the same header, sidebar, and footer that's seen on the home page.

The Aspire theme and the Concept theme, shown in Figure 3.60 and Figure 3.61 respectively, both showcase well-designed page templates. The main elements are all addressed: a uniform header, sidebar, footer (not shown), and page content area. Notice the particular care given to the appearance of subheadings, images, lists, and the like. Publishers are able to use these elements easily within their pages, making them fit seamlessly with the rest of their site.

Aspire

HOME   ABOUT   SERVICES ▾   PORTFOLIO   BLOG   CONTACT

This is an optional page-headline you can use easily!

GREAT USES OF COLOR & SPACE IN MODERN WEB DESIGN

July 28th, 2009 | News | Brandon R Jones | 23 Comments

Aspire has been designed with more than just a basic *website template* in mind. It's been carefully built from the ground up, featuring custom typography, state of the art jQuery plugins, and a rock-solid code base. In short, this will be one of the best sites that you'll find available, ever. Save time and money; start up your next site with Aspire and never look back.

Donec adipisin lacinia adipiscing. Nulla lorem diam, tempor et consectetur vehicula dignissim ac erat. Nunc eu nisi non ipsum semper accumsan vita accumsan libero. Sed pharetra elit lobortis diam rhoncus suscipit. Inferis lorem ipsum dolorem sit.

Cras posuere, ligula accumsan dapibus pretium, nulla justo imperdiet enim, at facilisis lacus orci at lectus. Suspendisse potenti. Sed justo augue, commodo vitae dapibus sit amet, faucibus vel magna. Morbi vulputate vulputate lacus id accumsan. Mauris risus mauris, porttitor ac vestibulum sit amet, semper eget turpis. Proin vulputate, nibh at tempor rutrum, nunc lectus euismod lectus, sed luctus velit est malesuada risus. Ut mauris lorem, tempor sit amet rhoncus eget, volutpat vel lorem. Nulla sodales sodales nisi a interdum. Pellentesque viverra pulvinar magna.

Ready for Action, Right out of the Box!

Aenean tincidunt pharetra leo. Curabitur euismod sollicitudin elit. Donec faucibus lacus nec sapien. Aliquam ipsum nisi, scelerisque et, commodo nec, consectetur vel, tellus. Lorem ipsum dolor sit amet, consectetur adipiscing elit. Nunc ut nisi sed diam viverra porttitor. Donec in urna nunc, eget vestibulum risus. In cursus vestibulum nunc, eget viverra nibh sodales ultrices. Proin at diam interdum neque placerat suscipit. Sed egestas consectetur magna vitae rutrum. Duis a rutrum ligula. Nulla laoreet mollis tellus, et malesuada magna congue id. Nullam elementum, erat id eleifend posuere, sapien velit tincidunt massa. Proin at diam interdum neque placerat suscipit. Sed egestas consectetur magna vitae rutrum. Duis a rutrum ligula. Nulla laoreet mollis tellus, et malesuada magna congue id. Nullam elementum, erat id eleifend posuere,

AFFILIATES

themeforest
Site Templates and Themes

graphicriver
Awesome Stock Graphics

flashden
Stock Flash Files

audiojungle
Your Site for Music Loops

SEARCH

Enter Your Search Term...

SPONSOR

ARSENAL.
Professional Design Weapons

CHOOSE YOUR WEAPON

Figure 3.60. Smart design in the Aspire theme's standard page template

concept✳

HOME   ABOUT   SERVICES   MEDIA   CONTACT US   BLOG

Learn How Concept Works For You.

This is a great place to grab viewers' attention & tell them a little about what you do.

Overview of Wordpress Pages

This is an example of a WordPress page, you can create and edit as many of these pages as you'd like in a matter of minutes. It's easy and fun to create content, and if you ever want to change it, you have full control over making edits and changes. Pages are considered to be more or less "fixed" pieces of content within this theme, where as Blog Posts are something that I anticipate you'll be making updates to on a frequent basis. Whether you want to release content as a Blog Post or a Page, it's incredibly easy to do. Try it out for yourself, I'll be happy to help you out if you run into problems!

You'll also notice that you can have "sub-pages" that show up underneath a "parent" page. It's easy to create these sub-pages, and the theme automatically lists them in the dropdown menu for you. It's really that easy!

- Full page control, including custom headlines and sub-headlines for each page.
- Pre-styled content for all content types, including images, bold, italic, bullets, etc.
- Sidebar are easy to customize through Wordpress Widgets.
- Contact forms, search forms, and all major Wordpress content comes standard.

The Custom Admin Panel

I've taken the time to create a custom admin panel that allows you to change pretty much every major part of this theme that you can imagine. Included in the admin panel is full control over the site logo, the homepage content, navigation & footer pages, copyright information, the homepage callout block, and so much more!

GRAPHIC RIVER

Your Choice for ▸
Layered Photoshop
Vector Graphics
Icons & Add-ons

Search

Search

Our Mission Statement

Lorem ipsum dolor sit amet, consectetur adipiscing elit. Mauris in urna et urna bibendum cursus. Mauris nunc. Aenean vitae elit. In consequat, nisi eu imperdiet convallis, nisi ligula vulputate erat, id gravida arcu dui vel turpis.

Ut commodo augue vitae diam. Etiam quis magna ac elit rhoncus pretium. Praesent volutpat suscipit nulla. Sed elementum purus quis lectus.

Contact Us

Figure 3.61. The Concept theme's default page template

The Single Post Template

The single post template is used to display an individual blog post in its entirety. Where a page template typically only displays the page content, the single post template will usually show a lot of the metadata associated with the post, such as tags, categories, trackbacks (a type of linkback), comments, and the like.

Remember that while The Loop will often only display an excerpt from the post on your list pages, the single post template will display it in full. Some of the customizations you can implement may take the form of custom post images, separately styled pull-quotes, lists of related articles, and unique templates for different types or categories of posts. Let's take a look at a complete blog post template in Figure 3.62. This example of a single post template comes from the Spectrum theme by WooThemes.[6]

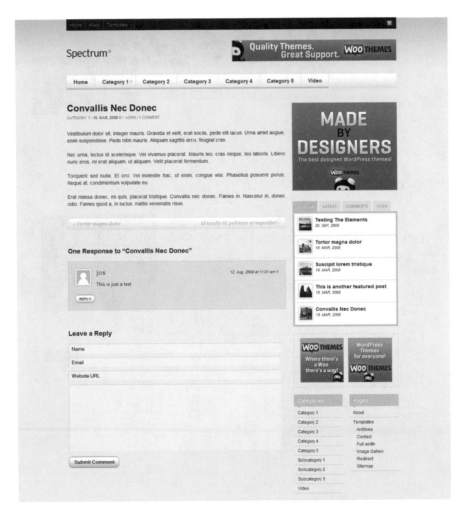

Figure 3.62. Just one example from the spectrum of single post themes available

---

[6] http://woothemes.com

The Archive, Author, Category, and Tag Page Templates

WordPress uses these templates to display lists of posts that are filtered on some criterion; this can be a category, tag, author, or date. As you'll see in the section called "Quick-and-dirty Template Hierarchy Reference" in Chapter 5, if your theme lacks a category, author, or tag template, the standard date-based archive template will be used to display those pages. This is often sufficient, as the needs of all those page types are very similar. However, you may wish to give one or more of these templates a specific style, and WordPress gives you the flexibility to do that.

These templates are very flexible, and there are a number of ways you can use them to present the posts. Figure 3.63 shows one possibility, from the SitePoint blogs.

Figure 3.63. The category archive on the SitePoint blogs displays excerpts of each post

The Search Results Page

This template handles the task of delivering results for search queries entered by the user. And don't worry: there's no requirement for you to know anything about search algorithms—WordPress does the hard work for you! All you have to decide on is how to display the results. The design for this page is likely to be similar to the archive template—after all, you're displaying a list of posts—but you also need to account for any other form of content that might be returned, like authors, categories, or pages.

It's worthwhile considering customizations that make the search page more helpful to users by showing additional content that might be relevant to a search query. For instance, let's check out the search results page from the ThemeShaper site in Figure 3.64. Note that the sidebar contains a bunch of suggested posts, in case the searcher failed to find what they were looking for.

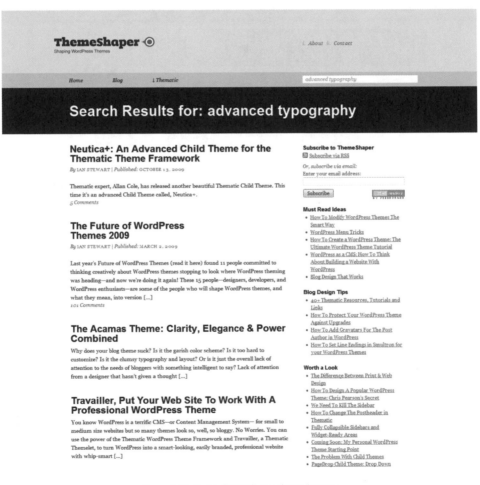

Figure 3.64. ThemeShaper's search results page

The 404 Page

WordPress provides built-in handling of "page not found" (404) errors. Rather than just sending users back to where they came from, an effective 404 page will help users by including a search form to find the content they seek, and suggesting how to report the problem if they arrived via an internal link. You might also consider using this page to display popular content from the rest of the site—after all, there's no reason for them to leave the site right away!

Figure 3.65 and Figure 3.66 show some cleverly designed 404 error pages.

Figure 3.65. The 404 error page from WooThemes

DRATS. IT'S NOT HERE.
LOOKS LIKE THAT URL DOESN'T WORK.
YOU MIGHT TRY A DIFFERENT ONE.
WE'VE GOT LOTS.

You can
Go home, try again or search the site:

Or, take a look at Backstories or Bold Locals

Nerd info:
ERROR 404
File not found

Figure 3.66. A stylized 404 page from The Bold Italic[7]

---

[7] http://thebolditalic.com/

Standard Styling for HTML Elements

An often overlooked but crucial piece of the WordPress theme anatomy that should be addressed in the design phase is a standard HTML test page. This is just a regular WordPress page whose purpose is to test styling for all of the commonly used HTML elements: headings, paragraphs, form elements, lists, images, links, blockquotes, and so on, to ensure that they don't break the layout and that the styling is consistent with the rest of the theme.

The Canvas theme by WooThemes has a very thorough test page, shown in Figure 3.67. Note that the designers have taken care to include both ordered and unordered lists, as well as every level of heading; this is the level of detail you should aim for.

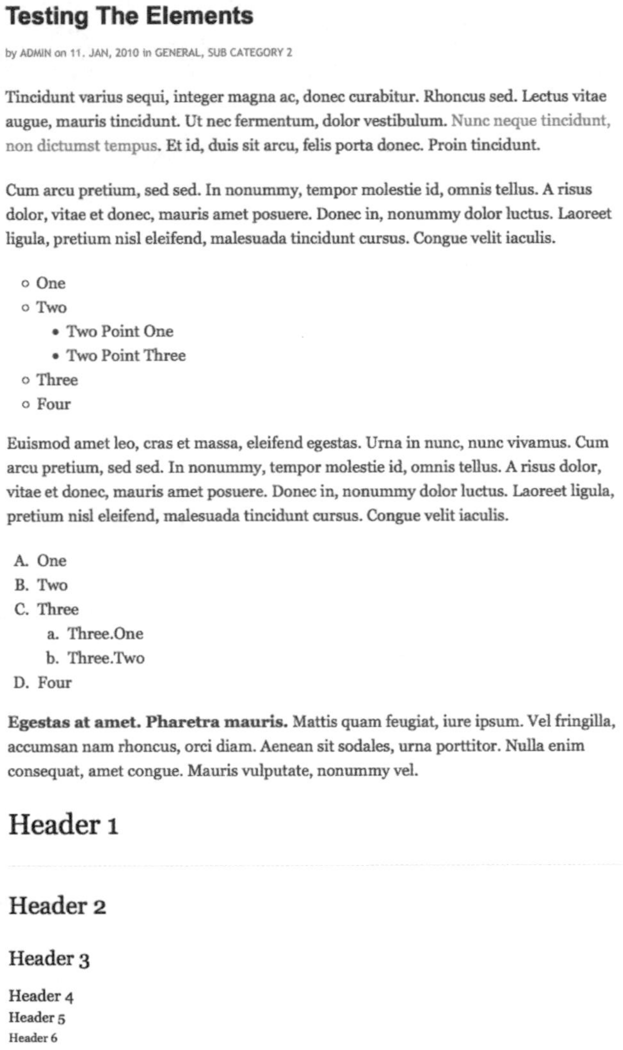

Testing The Elements

by ADMIN on 11. JAN, 2010 in GENERAL, SUB CATEGORY 2

Tincidunt varius sequi, integer magna ac, donec curabitur. Rhoncus sed. Lectus vitae augue, mauris tincidunt. Ut nec fermentum, dolor vestibulum. Nunc neque tincidunt, non dictumst tempus. Et id, duis sit arcu, felis porta donec. Proin tincidunt.

Cum arcu pretium, sed sed. In nonummy, tempor molestie id, omnis tellus. A risus dolor, vitae et donec, mauris amet posuere. Donec in, nonummy dolor luctus. Laoreet ligula, pretium nisl eleifend, malesuada tincidunt cursus. Congue velit iaculis.

- One
- Two
  - Two Point One
  - Two Point Three
- Three
- Four

Euismod amet leo, cras et massa, eleifend egestas. Urna in nunc, nunc vivamus. Cum arcu pretium, sed sed. In nonummy, tempor molestie id, omnis tellus. A risus dolor, vitae et donec, mauris amet posuere. Donec in, nonummy dolor luctus. Laoreet ligula, pretium nisl eleifend, malesuada tincidunt cursus. Congue velit iaculis.

A. One
B. Two
C. Three
   a. Three.One
   b. Three.Two
D. Four

Egestas at amet. Pharetra mauris. Mattis quam feugiat, iure ipsum. Vel fringilla, accumsan nam rhoncus, orci diam. Aenean sit sodales, urna porttitor. Nulla enim consequat, amet congue. Mauris vulputate, nonummy vel.

Header 1

Header 2

Header 3

Header 4

Header 5

Header 6

Figure 3.67. The HTML element test page from WooThemes' Canvas theme

Extra Features

It's worth contemplating further additional features during the design phase. Think of the traditional WordPress theme being like an anatomically correct body, and these extras as the cool cyborg parts. It's impossible to list all of the add-on features that are out there, but here are a few of the more popular ones.

Feature Sliders

Feature sliders are also called dynamic leaderboards, image sliders, carousels, content rotators, feature boxes, and probably a thousand other names. Regardless of what you choose to call it, its purpose is to highlight a selection of featured content. It usually shows up in a prominent location just below the site header and loops through the featured items, often making use of a JavaScript-powered effect.

There are several approaches to designing this sort of feature; two are highlighted in Figure 3.68 and Figure 3.69.

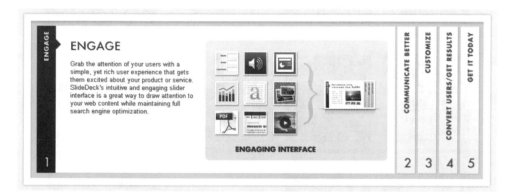

Figure 3.68. A sliding-panel feature box from the SlideDeck site

Figure 3.69. An image slider from the Atlantica Portfolio theme

Custom Page Templates

When designing for a WordPress theme, there's no reason to stop at just one standard page template. You can include a handful of extra page templates for publishers to pick from, should they want to make their content look a little different from page to page. Full-width templates, image gallery templates, and product templates are a few common ones.

Two alternative page templates from the same theme are shown in Figure 3.70 and Figure 3.71 (for comparison, we saw this theme's default page in Figure 3.60).

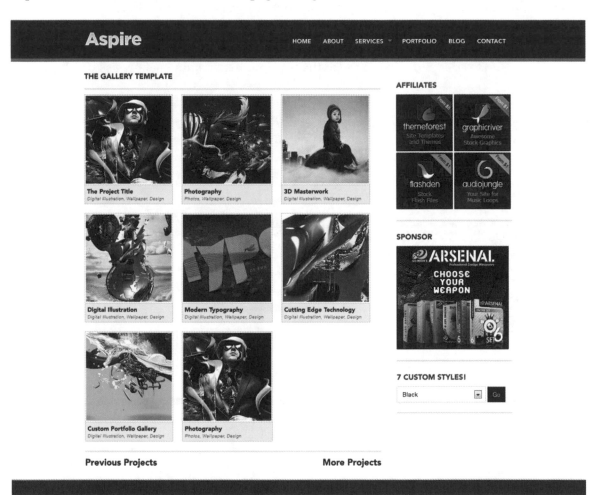

Figure 3.70. The Aspire theme's gallery template

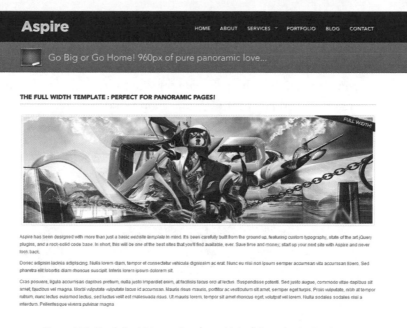

Figure 3.71. The full-width template (sans sidebar) from the Aspire theme

Advertising Blocks

An advertising block is simply a space that is predefined in your theme layout to be used for advertising or promotions. It's ideal for publishers who want to monetize their sites, but ad blocks also work just fine for standard bloggers for their own promotions.

Figure 3.72 shows a number of ad blocks placed in the sidebar and above the post content.

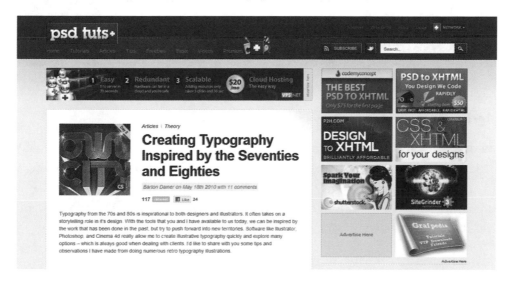

Figure 3.72. Psdtuts+ showcases several custom advertising spots in their site template

Lightboxes

A **lightbox** is essentially a JavaScript plugin that allows users to load large images inside a hovering container. This feature has grown steadily in popularity for photography and other image-dependent sites. When designing your theme, you should consider whether a lightbox would be appropriate for users. If you decide that it would be helpful, you're then faced with choosing what form it takes; this is where your script research from the last chapter will come in handy.

A standard example of a lightbox is shown in Figure 3.73. The prettyPhoto 3.0 plugin uses jQuery to present images in a gallery format. Note the thumbnail images along the bottom, as well as the arrow navigation.

Figure 3.73. The prettyPhoto 3.0 plugin

Social Media Add-ons

There is a wide variety of free plugins that allow users to include social media links in a WordPress site with little hassle. You can also bake these features directly into a theme, bypassing the need for a plugin altogether. Sidebar widgets and a list of social media buttons—for Twitter, Facebook, Digg, Delicious, and the like—at the bottom or top of a post are the most common ways of including such features, but you can also integrate them into the header or footer of your theme.

Figure 3.74 and Figure 3.75 are two examples of the kind of functionality you might consider; both are taken from the SitePoint blogs.

Figure 3.74. A sidebar social media widget

Figure 3.75. Social media sharing at the end of each post

Don't Leave Anything Out!

What you should take away from this chapter is the following: WordPress has a fixed number of parts for which you must design. In order to have a robust, usable theme, you need to account for *all* of these. Even if you have no plans to use each and every text element, form, or widget in your version of the theme, publishers using your theme might wish to—so to ignore designing for them will only prompt those publishers to go elsewhere because you fail to give them what they need.

Unlike a static website where you know exactly what elements you're designing for, it's important to account for everything in a WordPress theme. Make sure you look at all of the common HTML elements, WordPress widgets, and page templates when you're in the mockup stage.

Putting It All Together

Now that we've reviewed the core principles of design that affect a WordPress theme, as well as the basic elements that a theme is unable to live without, it's time for you to go to work on your own design. The next steps in the workflow of this book will walk you through actually building your theme, but I hope that you leave this chapter with a better impression of how WordPress themes are structured and designed. At their core, WordPress themes are a lot like any other website design. By following the fundamentals discussed in this chapter, you should be knocking out your own wicked themes in no time!

Theme Frameworks

by Raena Jackson Armitage

Once you have an idea of how you'd like your blog to appear, it's time to start hacking on the theme itself. Typically, a WordPress theme needs a number of core files to function—files for the index page, single posts, static pages, and all the bits and pieces that live inside, such as comments and sidebars. WordPress's core theme, Twenty Ten, contains 22 files in total, and that's excluding the images. There sure is a lot of work in there!

Savvy developers know that reinventing the wheel is for suckers, and when you want to start off on the right foot, it's often faster and easier to build on top of a framework. PHP developers have frameworks like CakePHP or CodeIgniter; Ruby geeks have Ruby on Rails; .NET developers have ASP.NET. The WordPress theme community is no exception—theme development frameworks have arisen to make it simpler for you to create your own theme.

WordPress theme development frameworks look just like regular themes—dare we say, even a little bit boring—yet underneath their modest facades lies powerful functionality that acts as a scaffold for your own theme development. In this chapter, we'll look at why frameworks are such a great idea, how to choose the best theme framework for you, and how to augment that framework with our own sexy styles and custom functionality.

Why use a framework?

I bet you're busy, right? You're probably also excited to start your theme development as soon as you can. And as your theme career grows, you'll appreciate anything that can help you save some time. Theme development frameworks are here to make your life a whole lot easier.

Frameworks provide markup, functional elements, and often some basic CSS, all of which you can use as a foundation for your own theme. For beginner themers, using a framework means that you can spend less time putting together your code, and more time concentrating on your design. It's also a great way to learn about how WordPress themes are put together, especially if you're fairly new to PHP.

Later on, once you've established yourself as a world-renowned WordPress theme rock star, you'll find that using a framework saves you time: you'll spend less time on doing the repetitive work that every theme requires, and more on the finer details of your newest masterpiece.

Child Themes: The Smart Way to Build on a Framework

Back in ye olden days, if you wanted to modify the output of a WordPress theme, you'd have to edit the theme directly. There were very few opportunities to alter a theme's markup or functionality without changing the template files. If the theme you started from was upgraded, you'd then have to spend time carefully integrating your alterations back into the newly updated original—hardly the most productive use of your time.

WordPress 2.7 changed all that when it introduced the concept of a **child theme**—a theme that extends on the capabilities of another theme. At a minimum, a child theme needs only a style sheet (**style.css**) within its own directory, and another theme specified as the parent. When WordPress builds a page, it'll take the style sheet from the child theme, and the templates from the parent theme.

But for the more adventurous, child themes can help you go even further, with two ways to override the behavior of the parent. There's an additional file, **functions.php**, that's available for adding your own code to the theme. What's more, template files stored within the child theme's directory will override those of the parent. This means that if you'd like to make changes to the parent theme's markup or functionality, all you need to do is write a custom function, or make your own version of the relevant template—and voilà, complete control.

Here's the best bit: while the WordPress community has developed a number of feature-rich frameworks especially for this purpose, any theme can act as a parent. If your favorite theme permits modification in its license, you're free to go right ahead and use it as a framework for your lovely new theme, without editing the original in any way.

There's nothing to prevent you from directly modifying a theme framework, if that's what floats your boat, but the smart money's on using a child theme as often as you can. Whenever your parent theme's developer makes an update to their theme, updating yours is as simple as installing the fresh version of the parent. Your child theme will be instantly updated at the same time, meaning that you spend less time worrying about incorporating your changes.

In this chapter, we'll be keeping a very important maxim in mind: hands off the parent theme! It's the cleanest, simplest way to build on a theme and avoid tripping over your own toes.

How do I choose a great framework?

As I mentioned earlier in this chapter, you can use any theme as a framework—providing, of course, that its license permits you to do so. That often means that a premium—or paid—theme is a poor choice for anyone who wants to distribute their themes for free. Here are some important points to examine.

Clean, semantic HTML

A theme with valid, semantic HTML means that it'll be a breeze to style up your theme with your own CSS. If your prospective theme has a demo page, run it through the W3C validator[1] and see what falls out. You should also keep an eye out for plenty of class hooks for you to hang your CSS on, as this will make your job much easier when it comes time to create your child theme.

CSS examples

A good framework will ideally come with some minimal CSS you can use as a starter for your own styling. A great framework will have a number of layouts available for you to use; ideally, it will also have different stylistic concerns such as typography, color, and layout placed in separate files, making it simple for you to pick and choose from the defaults.

SEO benefits

If you've dreamed of seeing your theme on thousands of popular blogs, you can bet that SEO will be uppermost in those bloggers' minds; it should be right up there in yours, too. Your framework's markup should follow good SEO practices, such as a sensible use of headings and semantic elements, descriptive `title` elements, and good use of `meta` elements.

Widget-ready

Your framework should include plenty of places for WordPress widgets. Your users will be less than impressed if your theme only permits widgets in sidebars. Choosy bloggers look for themes that support widgets above and below posts, in headers and footers, and indeed anywhere they can squeeze in their favorite gadgets and goodies.

---

[1] http://validator.w3.org/

Plays well with plugins

Your choice of framework should, ideally, play nicely with popular plugins. Some frameworks already include CSS for the most popular plugins, and at the very least, the framework developer should have tested the theme on a blog with plenty of plugins installed.

Documentation and support

A good theme framework will have documentation and an avenue for support, whether that's a forum, wiki, mailing list, or even a support ticket system. Take a look around and see what the community's like—are they helpful angels or cranky trolls? This is especially true if you're buying a paid theme; why drop all that cash for shabby or non-existent support?

Frameworks Worth Checking Out

Although any theme could conceivably be used as a framework, some notable examples have been designed especially for this purpose. We'll take a look at these now, as well as some child themes that have been created from them.

Freebies

Here are just a few of the great free frameworks on offer.

Thematic

Ian Stewart's Thematic, shown in Figure 4.1, is one of the best-known theme frameworks out there, and for good reason: it boasts thousands of users, it has been tested with dozens of popular plugins, and there's plenty of helpful, free community support. You can grab Thematic from ThemeShaper,[2] which is also home to a huge collection of tutorials about building child themes, as well as creating your own framework.

The Thematic Theme Framework

Just another WordPress weblog

| About | Element Examples | Example Images | Example Page |

A paginated post

By IAN STEWART | *Published:* APRIL 7, 2008

Lorem ipsum sensibus eleifend reprehendunt ex nam, vocent recusabo omittantur ei nam. Cum te altera numquam, in dicta corpora mel. Verear iisque theophrastus ex vix, volutpat evertitur disputando eu mel. Sed at lorem legere electram. Id duo fabellas ullamcorper consectetuer, vel quot malorum no! Has eu mollis iracundia.

The Thematic Demo Site
You're looking at the Thematic Demo Site. You can read more about the Thematic Theme and Download it from the Thematic Page on ThemeShaper.

To search, type and hit enter

Figure 4.1. A plain Thematic demo, using the default styles

[2] http://www.themeshaper.com/

Thematic child themes are plentiful: Figure 4.2, Figure 4.3, andFigure 4.4 show just how flexible this framework can be.

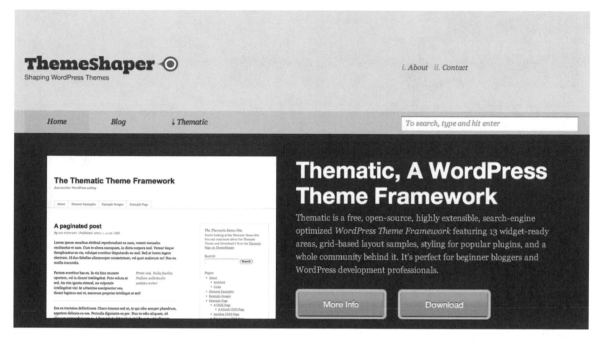

Figure 4.2. ThemeShaper uses a Thematic child theme

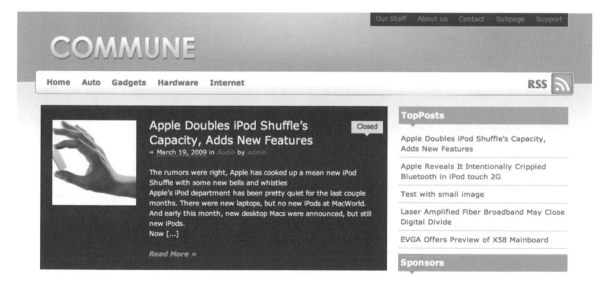

Figure 4.3. Commune, by Cristian Antohe[3]

---

[3] http://www.cozmoslabs.com/2009/04/07/green-anyone-try-commune-thematic-child-theme/

Figure 4.4. The Neutica+[4] child theme, by co-author Allan Cole

Hybrid

Justin Tadlock's Hybrid, shown in Figure 4.5, boasts plenty of documentation and support, and it's free and open source. You'll also find a collection of language translations, plenty of child themes to download and try, and Hybrid-specific plugins to enhance your use of this excellent free theme. Access to an extensive collection of in-depth tutorials and forums costs a reasonable US$25.

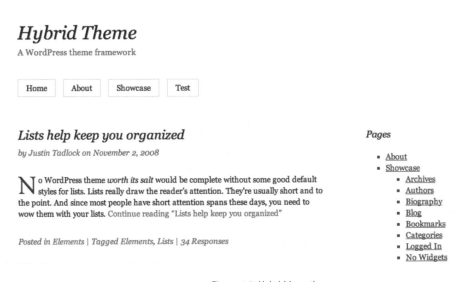

Figure 4.5. Hybrid in action

You can download Hybrid from Theme Hybrid.[5] While you are there, take a look at some of the lovely child theme examples by Justin; screenshots from two of them can be seen in Figure 4.6 and Figure 4.7.

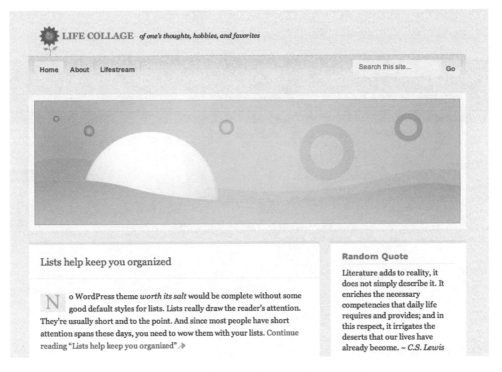

Figure 4.6. Share your thoughts with the world, with Life Collage

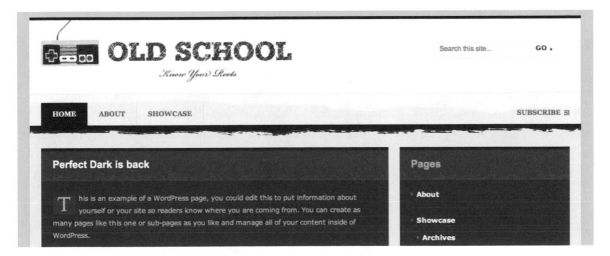

Figure 4.7. It's fun, it's hip, it's Old School

[5] http://themehybrid.com/

Carrington

CrowdFavorite's Carrington[6] framework is open source, and comes in four flavors: one with some graphic design laid in (Figure 4.8), one with no markup at all, one designed especially for mobile devices, and plain old vanilla. There's official and community support available, and plenty of documentation for the curious coder.

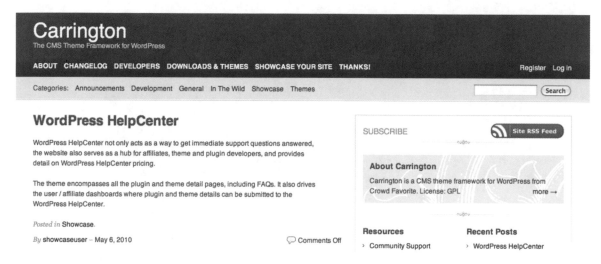

Figure 4.8. The blogger- and developer-friendly Carrington Blog

Paid Frameworks

These paid frameworks come with stacks of bells and whistles, a strong enterprise and SEO focus, and premium support.

Thesis

The Thesis framework from DIY Themes[7] promises to put an end to all your SEO worries, with plenty of options for end users and professional theme developers alike. In Thesis, you make modifications to a custom CSS and functions file within the theme itself, rather than using the child theme method mentioned above, but it's still a rock-solid framework nonetheless. At the time of writing, Thesis is $87 for personal use and $164 for developers, and there's a thriving marketplace for Thesis skins.[8] The default Thesis skin is shown in Figure 4.9.

---

[6] http://carringtontheme.com/
[7] http://diythemes.com/
[8] http://thesisthemes.com/

Figure 4.9. The rock-solid Thesis framework

Thesis drives a number of popular blogs; check out some of its high-profile users in Figure 4.10 and Figure 4.11 below.

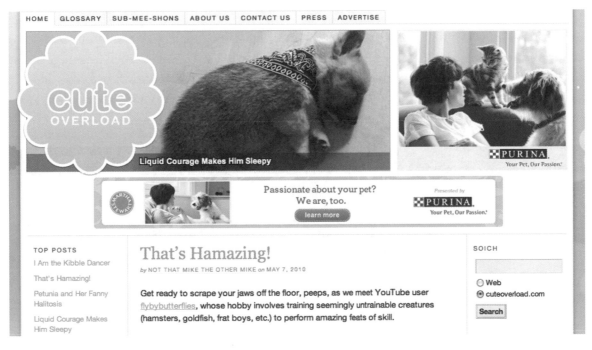

Figure 4.10. Cute Overload—for the finest in cute imagery

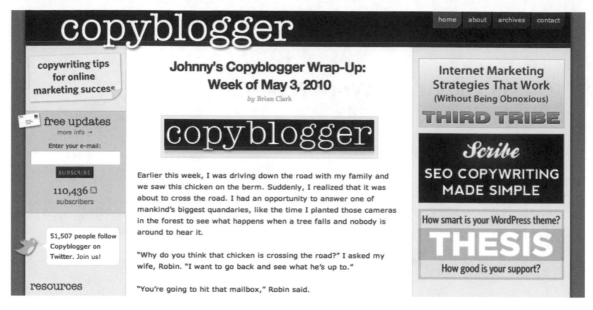

Figure 4.11. The compelling content of CopyBlogger

Genesis

StudioPress's Genesis framework[9] provides a plain, serviceable theme with numerous included layouts, and requires only a little CSS loving to really shine. Some Genesis-specific widgets help extend this theme well beyond alternative offerings. It's US$59.95 for your own use, and there's an official Genesis theme marketplace to sell your child themes. Figure 4.12 and Figure 4.13 show some of the cool variations you can achieve with the Genesis framework.

Figure 4.12. Viewing the Genesis theme demo

[9] http://www.studiopress.com/

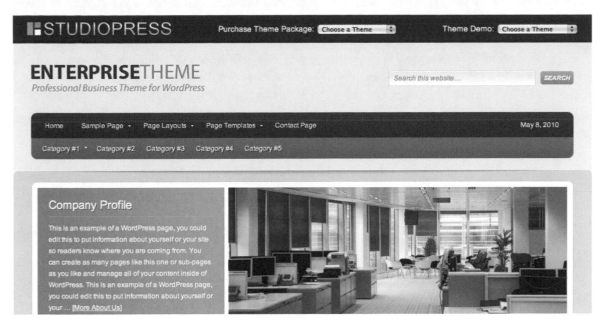

Figure 4.13. This Genesis child theme is truly enterprising

So which framework is the best?

C'mon, SitePoint, just tell us which is the best!

Well, the best theme framework for you to use is, of course, entirely up to you and your needs. In fact, you might decide that none of them are right for you, and that you'd rather roll your own. Whatever works for you!

For our part, we will work through the next four chapters using the free Thematic framework. It produces some terrific markup full of semantic classes to help you work wonders with CSS, and has an SEO-friendly presentation and plenty of possibilities for adding your own custom code. It's been created especially for the child theme method we have recommended in this book, and it is designed with theme developers in mind. It's also free, which makes it easy for you to play along at home with the examples from this chapter.

Building a Simple Child Theme

Enough theory—I bet you're absolutely champing at the bit to start on your theme. Let's make a simple child theme.

Preparing Your Canvas

To start with, we will assume that you have already grabbed a copy of WordPress to use for theme development and testing, as suggested in Chapter 1. We'll also assume that you've populated your development blog with some dummy content.

What's all this about dummy content?

It's important to road test your theme with a good variety of content. Of course, if you have your own WordPress blog, you could export your blog's content as a WordPress export file (from **Tools > Export**), and import it into your dev blog (by navigating to **Tools > Import**, and then clicking on the **WordPress** link). Another option is to create that test content by hand, ensuring that you've included lots of different content: large and small images, ordered and unordered lists, blockquotes, paginated posts, and the like.

But the fastest way of all is to grab some dummy content and import it. A good way to do so is with WordPress's very own theme unit testing file, which you can grab from the Codex[10]—it'll fill your blog with posts of all shapes and sizes, pages, tags, categories, and even some attachments. You could also try the WP Dummy Content plugin,[11] which can add and remove zillions of posts with a few easy button presses.

Grab a copy of Thematic from its download page,[12] or use the theme browser in your WordPress installation, and install it in your WordPress **wp-content/themes** directory. Feel free to go ahead and activate it as your theme right now—it's a great opportunity to see how a default Thematic theme looks and works.

View the source of your blog's home page, and you'll see what makes Thematic's markup great: it's stuffed with useful `class` names, `id`s, microformats, and more. Here's the `body` element of my test blog:

```
<body class="wordpress y2010 m05 d01 h14 home blog not-singular
  loggedin mac firefox ff3">
```

And here's one for the `div` element that surrounds the first post on the page:

```
<div id="post-86" class="hentry p1 post publish author-raena
  category-uncategorized untagged comments-open pings-open
  y2008 m04 d01 h11 alt slug-test-post">
```

Hey, we did warn you that it was stuffed! I bet you're wondering what all these `class`es are for, and I'm glad you asked. What makes Thematic's HTML output so useful for themers is that there's usually a `class` for any purpose you can think of, and that means you can achieve a lot of cool effects without the need to modify the templates in any way. Imagine you wanted to decorate your post headers with a little heart every time you used the tag "love." Well, that's easy, because Thematic creates a `class` for every tag and puts it on the post's `div`.

---

[10] http://codex.wordpress.org/Theme_Development_Checklist#Theme_Unit_Test
[11] http://wordpress.org/extend/plugins/wp-dummy-content/
[12] http://themeshaper.com/thematic/

For our sample post above we had an `untagged` `class` because the post had no tags attached to it, but for posts that have tags you'll see `class`es that look like `tag-tagname`. So we're looking to target posts with `class` `tag-love`:

```
.post .tag-love .entry-title {
  background: url(heart.gif) center left no-repeat
}
```

Do you need the first post on your home page to have bigger text? Easy! Thematic gives every post a post number `class`, and there's a `home` `class` on the `body` tag when you're viewing the home page. So we want to do this:

```
body.home .p1 { font-size: 1.5em }
```

Should the header be taller on a specific page? Thematic shows you a `class` for every post or page's ID, so it's a cinch:

```
body.pageid-14 #header { height: 500px; }
```

Suffering from a terrible case of the IE6 blues? Put away those dodgy hacks; Thematic's browser, version, and platform `class`es have you covered:

```
body.ie6 #branding {
  /* do IE 6 specific stuff here */
}
```

Take some time to look through Thematic's markup and learn about some of the useful `class`es it provides. Chances are that Thematic's dynamic `id`s and `class`es will allow you make some very specific style changes without the need to hack away at the markup.

At this point, it's also worth looking inside the **thematic** directory to see what makes it tick. Let's check it out: we see a number of PHP template files, some directories, a readme file, and, of course, the CSS for this theme. Most of the filenames should be fairly self-explanatory: the **header.php** file looks after header logic, **post.php** relates to how posts are displayed, and so forth. Inside the **library** folder, you'll find a collection of handy helpers—more CSS, JavaScript, and PHP files—that Thematic uses to work some of its magic. We'll find these useful later on, but if you're the curious type, feel free to poke around and see some of the code that drives this theme.

And hey, what's that at the bottom there? Thematic has even provided its own sample child theme to start us off on the right foot, conveniently called **thematicsamplechildtheme**. Inside it, there's a **style.css** file, a **functions.php** file, and a handy readme, inviting us to kick-start our child theme with these files. I think we'll do just that!

Creating Your Child Theme

Copy the **thematicsamplechildtheme** directory back up to the **wp-content/themes** directory, and give it a new name. I plan to call my new child theme "Wicked," so I've named this folder appropriately: **wicked**.

Next, we'll need to make some changes to the theme information, which is all stored within the theme's **style.css** file. Open it up in your favorite text editor, and take a look at what's there:

chapter_04/v1/wicked/style.css (excerpt)

```
/*
Theme Name: A Thematic Child Theme
Theme URI:
Description: Use this theme to start your Thematic Child Theme development.
Author: Ian Stewart
Author URI: http://themeshaper.com/
Template: thematic
Version: 1.0
Tags: Thematic
.
Thematic is © Ian Stewart http://themeshaper.com/
.
*/
⋮
```

What's happening here? Well, that big comment block at the very beginning of the file performs a very important job: it defines the theme's title, author, URI, description, tags, and version number. This information appears alongside each theme in your WordPress installation's **Appearance > Themes** panel, shown in Figure 4.14.

There are two items which are absent from the Manage Themes panel, however. The line beginning with `Template:` tells WordPress that Thematic is our parent theme, so it should use the templates from Thematic by default. The other line with the copyright statement is also excluded from the WordPress admin section; this is a place to put comments, instructions, or even a good knock-knock joke—anything you like.

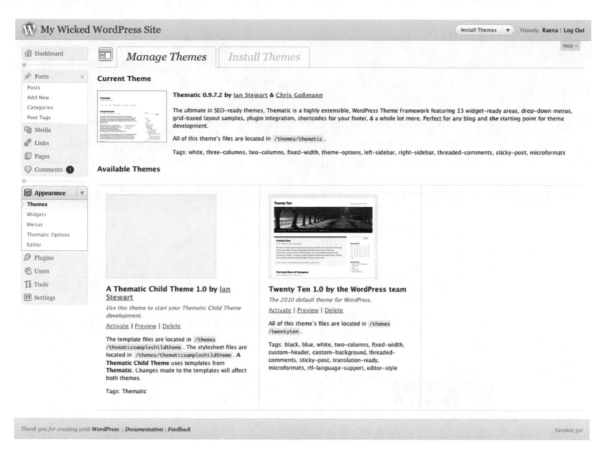

Figure 4.14. The Manage Themes panel in WordPress 3, showing Twenty Ten and Thematic

Let's personalize this theme's info now. It's okay if you've yet to decide on a name or a description; we can go back and change this whenever we like, but for now, defining a name at the very least is a good start:

chapter_04/v2/wicked/style.css (excerpt)

```
/*
Theme Name: Wicked Theme
Theme URI: http://example.com/themes/wicked
Description: A Thematic child theme that's just for kicks.
Author: Raena Jackson Armitage
Author URI: http://example.com/themes
Template: thematic
Version: 0.1
Tags: Thematic, three-columns, blue, grey, gray
.
This theme is © 2010 Raena Jackson Armitage.
.
*/

⋮
```

Keep It Compact!

Line breaks matter to WordPress and these items belong on one line each. If your description is so long that it requires a new paragraph, you might want to think about editing it.

Now that we've named our theme, let's address the Manage Themes panel once more. If you've performed each of these steps correctly, you'll see your theme sitting alongside any other installed themes, with your name, description, and additional information as shown in Figure 4.15.

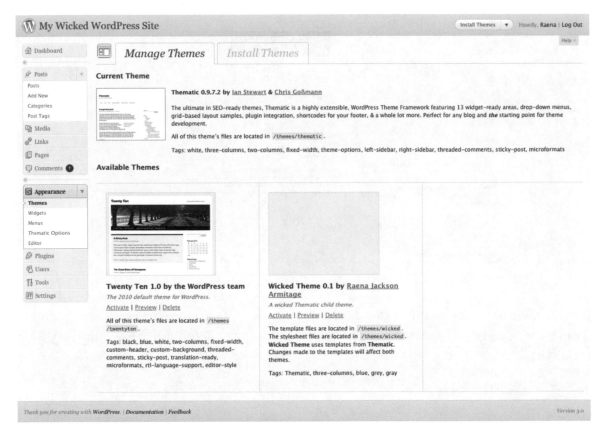

Figure 4.15. Hey, that's my theme!

All seems in order here. Let's activate our theme and start styling it up!

Looking Stylish

For now, we'll start by adjusting the CSS to suit our design a little better. Thematic helpfully provides a bunch of nifty reset styles, prepackaged layouts, typography, and other CSS helpers; if you look further down in the **styles.css** file, you'll see that they've been imported into our sample child theme. Here's what the rest of the theme's **style.css** looks like:

chapter_04/v2/wicked/style.css *(excerpt)*

```
      ⋮

/* Reset browser defaults */
@import url('../thematic/library/styles/reset.css');

/* Apply basic typography styles */
@import url('../thematic/library/styles/typography.css');

/* Apply a basic layout */
@import url('../thematic/library/layouts/2c-r-fixed.css');

/* Apply basic image styles */
@import url('../thematic/library/styles/images.css');

/* Apply default theme styles and colors */
/* It's better to actually copy over default.css into this file
(or link to a copy in your child theme) if you're going to do
anything outrageous */
@import url('../thematic/library/styles/default.css');

/* Prepare theme for plugins */
@import url('../thematic/library/styles/plugins.css');
```

 ### Don't Sweat the Style Sheet!

The ins and outs of how to work with CSS are beyond the scope of this book—we figure that if you're interested in WordPress theming, you already have some understanding of how to use CSS. For an introduction to the wild and woolly world of the style sheet, it's hard to go past *Build Your Own Web Site the Right Way using HTML and CSS*, 2nd edition (Melbourne: SitePoint, 2008) and the handy online reference text, SitePoint CSS Reference.[13]

While the basic design Thematic provides is … well, nice, it certainly falls short in the glamor stakes. Let's make some changes to the typography, colors, and layout.

The first change is easy: at the moment this theme places a sidebar on the right, but I'd prefer it on the left. Thematic's **library/layouts** folder provides a bunch of layouts we could apply to our theme: two-column left (**2c-l-fixed.css**) or right (**2c-r-fixed.css**), three-column with a sidebar on either side of the main content (**3c-fixed.css**), or three-column with both sidebars right (**3c-r-fixed.css** and **3c-r-fixed-primary.css**, which differ in the order of the sidebars).

Changing the default is as easy as picking out the one we want, and changing the reference to it in our **style.css** file. In this case, I want **2c-r-fixed.css** to move my sidebar onto the left:

---

[13] http://reference.sitepoint.com/css/

```
/* Apply a basic layout */
@import url('../thematic/library/layouts/2c-l-fixed.css');
```

Feeling kind of penned in?

Of course, if none of these imported styles suit your ideas, you're free to remove the `@import` statements and build your own layout, typography, or default reset style sheets. Remember, you're in control!

Next, let's think about color. Did you notice the helpful little comment about **default.css** in the code example above? It's reminding us to copy the **default.css** file to our own theme if we plan to do anything outrageous.

What we're about to do is hardly outrageous, but the advice to copy the file over is solid: let's do that now, and change our `@import` statement to reflect its new location. Copy the **default.css** file from the **thematic** directory into your child theme's directory, then change the `@import` accordingly. Feel free to change its name; you may want to leave yourself a comment to remind yourself that it's a copy of the original. For the purposes of my Wicked theme, I've renamed the file **newstyles.css**:

```
/* Apply default theme styles and colors
-- This is a copy of the Thematic default.css */
@import url('newstyles.css');
```

Thematic's CSS and the GPL

Thematic is released under the General Public License; if you copy its CSS for use in your child theme your CSS will also be bound by the terms of this license. While this may pose no problem for you (plenty of successful commercial themes are GPL-licensed), if you plan on distributing your theme and would prefer a more restrictive license for your clients (see the section called "Dual Licensing" in Chapter 8), you'll need to write your own style sheet from scratch.

The file is a big one—too long to reproduce in this book—but here's an excerpt from it. Take your time and look over it carefully; you'll see that selectors are grouped according to purpose, and there's a style for just about any element you think you might use. We'll start by splashing a bit of paint on the theme's header; we're looking for a section helpfully marked =Header. Here's what we find there:

```
#header {
  z-index:2;
}
```

```
#branding {
  padding:88px 0 44px 0;
}

#blog-title {
  font-family:Arial,sans-serif;
  font-size:34px;
  font-weight:bold;
  line-height:40px;
}

#blog-title a {
  color:#000;
  text-decoration:none;
}

#blog-title a:active,
#blog-title a:hover {
  color: #FF4B33;
}

#blog-description {
  color:#666;
  font-size:13px;
  font-style:italic;
}
```

Changing the colors is simple: I've chosen a dark blue for the background, and that means the text and link colors also need to change:

chapter_04/v3/wicked/newstyles.css *(excerpt)*

```
#header {
  z-index:2;
  background: #07426c;
}

⋮

#blog-title a {
  color:#fff;
  text-decoration:none;
}

#blog-title a:active,
#blog-title a:hover {
  color: #f47920;
}
```

```
#blog-description {
  color:#eee;
  font-size:13px;
  font-style:italic;
}
```

How's that looking? Let's find out: the result is shown in Figure 4.16.

Figure 4.16. Looking sharp

As I add and adjust more styles, my theme begins to take shape. We'll omit all the gory details from this book, but if you're curious to see what I came up with, feel free to dive into the code archive [14] and examine my CSS.

Keep Poking Away at Those Styles

Seems reasonably straightforward, right? It's simply a matter of examining the theme's markup, and finding a way to bring your design to life with your sharp CSS skills. With some keen CSS, and a few hours' poking, prodding, and refreshing, you should have a sharp-looking template. You can see what I achieved in Figure 4.17 using only CSS changes. You can poke through the styles I used in the **v4** folder in the code archive for this chapter.[15]

---

[14] Grab the archive from http://sitepoint.com/books/wordpress1/code.php
[15] The header image is licensed under Creative Commons [http://creativecommons.org/licenses/by-sa/2.0/] by Flickr user Seo2. [http://www.flickr.com/photos/seo2/]

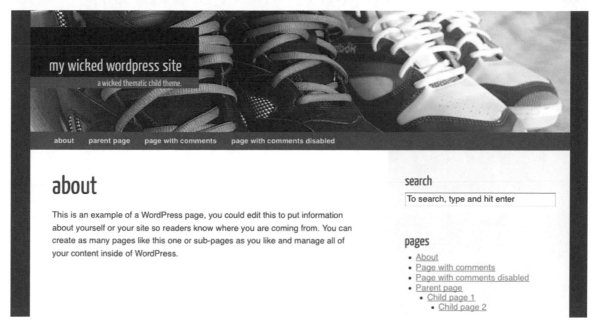

Figure 4.17. Wicked!

A Frame to Work With

We've learned how easy it is to boost our theme development efforts with a theme framework—using a framework will save us heaps of tedious setup time, leaving us free to dive into the fun part of making it all look great.

Many themers will find that simply modifying the CSS is all it takes to create a nifty, original child theme. But what if you want to spread your wings a little further? In the next chapter, we'll explore how to add more functionality to a theme.

Advanced Theme Construction

by Raena Jackson Armitage

In the previous chapter, we explored how to create a new child theme from the Thematic framework using a few files and some CSS smarts. Now you're probably wondering how to make that child theme work a bit harder for you and put your own stamp on it. If so, this is the chapter for you!

Before we start messing with code, however, it's time to reiterate what we learned in Chapter 4: hands off the parent theme! Even if you decide you absolutely detest the way a particular part of your parent theme works, and you're desperate to change it, it's best to avoid hacking the guts out of the parent theme. We have ways to modify it in a safe, simple fashion.

Understanding how to do so first requires some explanation of how WordPress thinks about your templates—here's the backstory.

How Templates Work

Template files are a blend of HTML and PHP and can contain your own code, as well as calls to WordPress's core functionality. When developing your theme, one of your main tasks will be to look through your parent theme's templates and find the places where the markup you want to modify is being generated. In order to do that you need to have some background knowledge of how WordPress templates work, so we'll start there.

When WordPress renders a page, it checks in the active theme's directory for the right template to use for the type of content it's going to display. How does it know which template file to pick? It depends on the type of page being rendered at the time, and which templates are available for use.

WordPress will check for template files with very specific names, in a very specific order, before finally falling back to **index.php**; this serves as a sort of catch-all for rendering pages when no particular templates are defined.

Quick-and-dirty Template Hierarchy Reference

Here's a quick reference to the filenames WordPress looks for when it renders each type of page.

Home Page

In WordPress 3.0, a blog administrator can specify whether to show the latest posts or a static page as the blog's home page. The templates WordPress looks for, in order, are:

1. **front-page.php**
2. **page.php** or **home.php**, depending on what was chosen in the blog's settings
3. **index.php**

WordPress 2.x lacks this feature, so the order will simply be:

1. **home.php**
2. **index.php**

Single Posts

1. **single-posttype.php**, where `posttype` represents one of WordPress 3.0's post types. For example, if your blog was about recipes, and you had a post type called Recipes, WordPress would look for a template called **single-recipes.php**.
2. **single.php**
3. **index.php**

Single Pages

1. WordPress will first look for a template specified in the page's template setting—more on this later.
2. **page-slug.php**, where `slug` is the slug specified on the page. For example, if you had a page called About, WordPress would first look for **page-about.php**.
3. **page-id.php**, being the numeric ID of the page. If your About page had an ID of 2, then the template WordPress would look for is **page-2.php**.
4. **page.php**
5. **index.php**

Attachments

1. **MIMEtype.php**, where `MIMEtype` represents the broad type of your attachment—like **audio.php**, **image.php**, **text.php**, or **video.php**

2. **attachment.php**
3. **index.php**

 What are mimes doing in WordPress?

On the Internet, the format of a piece of data, such as a document or a web page, is specified by a header called a MIME type. MIME stands for **Multipurpose Internet Mail Extension**, although MIME headers are in use for more than just mail. Common MIME types for familiar documents include `text/html` for HTML documents, `application/zip` for ZIP documents, `image/gif` for GIF images, and so on.

Category Archives

1. **category-slug.php**, where `slug` is the category's slug.
2. **category-id.php**, where `id` is the category's numeric ID.
3. **category.php**
4. **archive.php**
5. **index.php**

Tag Archives

1. **tag-slug.php**, where `slug` is the tag's slug.
2. **tag-id.php**, where `id` is the tag's numeric ID.
3. **tag.php**
4. **archive.php**
5. **index.php**

Taxonomy Archives

Custom taxonomies are new to WordPress 3, so these templates are never called by WordPress 2.

1. **taxonomy-taxonomyname-term.php**, where `taxonomyname` represents the slug of the custom taxonomy, and `term` represents that of the term. If your taxonomy was called Cheeses and your term was Brie, then WordPress will look for **taxonomy-cheese-brie.php** when listing items from that term.
2. **taxonomy-taxonomyname.php**, similar to the above, but without the term.
3. **taxonomy.php**
4. **archive.php**
5. **index.php**

Author Archives

1. **author-nicename.php**, where `nicename` is the author's username made suitable for URLs—all lowercase, with spaces transformed into hyphens. If an author's username was Kelly Steele, then the template WordPress would look for would be **author-kelly-steele.php** (WP3).
2. **author-id.php**, where the `id` is the author. If Kelly's ID were 3, then **author-3.php** would be the template WordPress would choose (WP3).
3. **author.php**
4. **archive.php**
5. **index.php**

Date-based Archives

1. **date.php**
2. **archive.php**
3. **index.php**

Search Pages

1. **search.php**
2. **index.php**

404 Page

1. **404.php**
2. **index.php**

That sure is a lot of stuff to remember. Fortunately, Rami from wp-tricks[1] has made a neat diagram[2] that explains the template hierarchy visually. You might like to print it and use it as a cheat sheet!

Always in Motion Is the Future

New versions of WordPress arrive roughly every three to four months, and new template names could be added to any of the upcoming releases. Check the WordPress Codex Template Hierarchy page[3] for the latest and greatest.

The Template Hierarchy and Child Themes

When you're using a child theme, the template hierarchy becomes a little more complex. WordPress will first look for the most specific template in your child theme, then to the parent, then back to

---

[1] http://www.wp-tricks.co.il/
[2] http://codex.wordpress.org/images/1/18/Template_Hierarchy.png
[3] http://codex.wordpress.org/Template_Hierarchy

the child for the next most specific, then back to the parent again—all the way down the line until it finally falls back on the parent's **index.php** file. Is your head spinning yet? Here's an example.

Let's say you have an FAQ page with a slug of `faq` and an ID of 12. WordPress will first check whether you've specified a template in the page's settings; if not, it checks for the following files in order:

1. the child theme's **page-faq.php**
2. the parent's **page-faq.php**
3. the child again for **page-12.php**
4. the parent's **page-12.php**
5. the child's **page.php** (Are we detecting a pattern here?)
6. the parent's **page.php**
7. the child's **index.php**
8. finally, the parent's **index.php**

Of course, WordPress can do all this in the blink of an eye.

Thematic's Templates

As we learned back in Chapter 4, Thematic is a great framework because it's packed with cool functionality. To best understand how to build on its templates, we should spend some time finding out how they're put together.

Let's take a look again inside Thematic's directory; you'll see a pile of template files, and if you were paying close attention to the previous section, many of these should be familiar to you:

- **404.php**
- **archive.php**
- **archives.php**
- **attachment.php**
- **author.php**
- **category.php**
- **comments.php**
- **footer.php**
- **functions.php**
- **header.php**
- **index.php**
- **links.php**
- **page.php**
- **search.php**
- **searchform.php**
- **sidebar-index-bottom.php**

- sidebar-index-insert.php
- sidebar-index-top.php
- sidebar-page-bottom.php
- sidebar-page-top.php
- sidebar-single-bottom.php
- sidebar-single-insert.php
- sidebar-single-top.php
- sidebar-subsidiary.php
- sidebar.php
- single.php
- tag.php

There's also a curious-looking directory, **library**, which is filled with directories for styles, languages, scripts, and so on. The most interesting subdirectory in there is **extensions**—it contains all the stuff that makes Thematic do the voodoo that it do. Erm, does. Here's what's inside:

- comments-extensions.php
- content-extensions.php
- discussion.php
- dynamic-classes.php
- footer-extensions.php
- header-extensions.php
- helpers.php
- shortcodes.php
- sidebar-extensions.php
- theme-options.php
- widgets-extensions.php
- widgets.php

The names of each of these files should give you a clue as to what they deal with: **footer-extensions.php** obviously relates to footers, **comments-extensions.php** to comments, and so on.

Building a Magazine-style Home Page

Now that we've acquired some understanding of how WordPress deals with templates, let's put that knowledge into practice and begin customizing our theme.

The default look and behavior of Thematic is, well, kind of bloggy—nothing against blogs, mind you, but we want our theme to have a bit more zing. Throughout the rest of this chapter, we'll modify the home page by ditching that sidebar, creating an area to list the excerpts and post thumbnails from a few of the most recent posts, and adding a homepage-specific footer element that repeats the page listing. We'll also add social media links and an author bio to each post, wherever it happens to be displayed.

Ditching That Sidebar

When you're working with a theme framework, the simple way to build your own theme template is to copy the relevant file from the parent and place it into your child theme. As we've just seen, when WordPress is rendering a page, it will check the child theme first, so any template we put in our child theme will override the equivalent template in Thematic. For our first trick, we want to remove the sidebar from the home page. When WordPress wants to render the home page, it will first check the settings to see whether the blog administrator has specified a page to act as the home page; otherwise, it will look for the **home.php** template.

Thematic lacks a **home.php** file to copy, but **index.php** will suit our purposes nicely as it currently includes all the page elements we want, as well as a list of recent posts. Copy it from Thematic, place it into your child theme, and rename it to **home.php**. Here's the new template in its entirety:

chapter_05/v1/wicked/home.php

```php
<?php

  // calling the header.php
  get_header();

  // action hook for placing content above #container
  thematic_abovecontainer();

?>

    <div id="container">

        <?php thematic_abovecontent(); ?>

        <div id="content">

          <?php

    // create the navigation above the content
    thematic_navigation_above();

    // calling the widget area 'index-top'
    get_sidebar('index-top');

    // action hook for placing content above the index loop
    thematic_above_indexloop();

    // action hook creating the index loop
    thematic_indexloop();
```

```php
        // action hook for placing content below the index loop
        thematic_below_indexloop();

        // calling the widget area 'index-bottom'
        get_sidebar('index-bottom');

        // create the navigation below the content
        thematic_navigation_below();

        ?>

            </div><!-- #content -->

            <?php thematic_belowcontent(); ?>

        </div><!-- #container -->
<?php

    // action hook for placing content below #container
    thematic_belowcontainer();

    // calling the standard sidebar
    thematic_sidebar();

    // calling footer.php
    get_footer();

?>
```

Were you expecting a bunch of HTML, curly braces, and a mess of `if` statements? All we have here is a couple of lonely `div` elements, and a whole lot of PHP function calls.

The reason for this is that Thematic templates are extremely modular—that **extensions** folder we noticed earlier is where much of the real action takes place. We'll delve deeper into what all these functions do and how to make sense of this sort of template later in the chapter. For now, let's focus on accomplishing our first task.

Looking at our freshly copied template, it's easy to see where the sidebar is coming from:

```php
// calling the standard sidebar
thematic_sidebar();
```

Removing it, of course, will be as simple as removing the call to the **thematic_sidebar**: feel free to remove or **comment out**[4] those two lines.

---

[4] Meaning wrap in comments, so as to temporarily disable it while keeping the ability to restore it easily.

Since we'd like the content to now span the width of the entire page, we'll need to modify the CSS applied to the main content column. We're importing Thematic's style sheets in our example, so there are two selectors that apply to the two divs: #container and #content, each specifying a width. We also learned back in Chapter 4 that Thematic loads up a bunch of classes on the body element, one of which we know will tell us we're on the home page.

You CSS whizzes have surely already figured this one out: we can alter the CSS in our child theme so that #container and #content have a greater width when they descend from a body with a class of home. To do that, simply insert the following styles into your **style.css** file:

chapter_05/v1/wicked/newstyles.css *(excerpt)*

```
/* =Homepage specific styles
----------------------------------------------------------------- */
body.home #container {
  float: none;
  margin: 0;
  width: 960px;
}
body.home #content {
  width: 900px;
  overflow: hidden;
  margin: 0 0 0 10px;
}
body.home .hentry {
  width: inherit;
}
⋮
```

Now, open your browser and take a look at your site's home page—you should find that the content occupies the entire width of the page, with nary a hint of a sidebar. And, if you navigate to any other page, you will see the sidebar reappear and the main content column take on its previous proportions.

Quite simple, right? But what we've just discovered is important: we've seen how easy it is to switch off an entire Thematic area without touching a single part of the parent theme's templates.

Including Files

Now that you have an idea of how the template hierarchy works and how to use it to your advantage, it's time to learn another key feature of WordPress themes. You've already seen a hint of this if you paid close attention to the list of Thematic's template files earlier. Some of them, like **header.php**, aren't particular to a specific page or type of page on the site. So when and how are they used? As it happens, WordPress provides a group of functions that include various common page components:

- `get_header` grabs **header.php**
- `get_footer` grabs **footer.php**
- `get_sidebar` grabs **sidebar.php**
- `get_searchform` grabs **searchform.php**—if this is missing, WordPress simply renders a default search form
- `comments_template` grabs **comments.php**

What's more, WordPress gives you two more useful ways to include goodies. First, you can optionally use those functions with an argument for the name: `get_header('custom')`, for example, will grab a file called **header-custom.php**. And, if you'd like to include other types of files that don't fit into any of those formats, you can use `get_template_part('partname')`, which grabs a template called **partname.php**.

The more PHP-inclined among you may be wondering why WordPress provides these functions when we have a perfectly good `include` method in PHP. I'm glad you asked. The reason why you might choose the `get_` functions over `include` is because they have some nifty, built-in dummy-proofing. Let's imagine your template needs to use a file called **footer-foobar.php**, which you'd call on like so:

```
get_footer('foobar');
```

Let's also imagine that some clumsy but well-meaning user deleted **footer-foobar.php**. If you'd used `include`, any page calling on it would show a couple of PHP errors that would tell every visitor that there's no such file or directory, making your theme's user look bad. With `get_footer`, however, WordPress will first check for **footer-foobar.php**, then try to include **footer.php** as a fallback. If **footer.php** is also missing, WordPress will give up quietly, leaving your poor user's reputation intact. Sweet!

If you really do have a need to use good old PHP includes, WordPress also provides you with constants called STYLESHEETPATH and TEMPLATEPATH for easy use with regular PHP `include` statements. TEMPLATEPATH is for use with standalone themes, and STYLESHEETPATH is for child themes. You'd use them like so:

```
include(STYLESHEETPATH . '/extrastuff/somefile.php');
```

Modifying the Footer

The next step in our custom home page layout is to modify the footer so that it includes a list of the blog's top-level pages. We now know that `get_footer` will look for a file called **footer.php** and include it. But if you call it with an argument, as in `get_footer('homepage')`, it will instead pull in **footer-homepage.php**. Near the bottom of **home.php**, you'll see where **home.php** calls on `get_footer`:

```
// calling footer.php
get_footer();
```

To call on another file instead, give it an argument:

```
// calling footer.php
get_footer('homepage');
```

Of course, this will do very little for us at the moment—we'll need to create **footer-homepage.php**. Again, copying from the parent theme is a great idea. We'll copy **footer.php** from Thematic, and place it into our child theme, renaming it **footer-homepage.php**. It looks like this:

```
</div><!-- #main -->

<?php

// action hook for placing content above the footer
thematic_abovefooter();

?>

  <div id="footer">

  <?php

  // action hook creating the footer
  thematic_footer();

  ?>

  </div><!-- #footer -->

<?php

// action hook for placing content below the footer
thematic_belowfooter();

if (apply_filters('thematic_close_wrapper', true)) {
  echo '</div><!-- #wrapper .hfeed -->';
}

<?php
```

```
// calling WordPress's footer action hook
wp_footer();

// action hook for placing content before closing the BODY tag
thematic_after();

?>


</body>
</html>
```

Around line 13, `thematic_footer` appears: this controls the display of the footer text, which you can set in the options panel Thematic provides to the WordPress admin section. We'll learn more about custom options panels and how you can create one for your child theme in Chapter 7.

Now, to put the list of pages in: WordPress's `wp_list_pages`[5] function will do exactly that. Most times when you find yourself wanting to include some additional content in your theme, WordPress will have a function ready to provide the information you need. Just have a look around the Codex: most functions have names that give a clear idea of what they do.

We could plop `wp_list_pages` right there in our new home page footer template, and it'd all work fine. But as a point of good housekeeping, it's a better idea to stash this away in our **functions.php** file. **functions.php** tends to serve as a catch-all for the custom functionality you add to your child theme. By storing our page list generator in there, we ensure that if we ever need to call on it in some other part of our template, we can find it easily and refer to it in a simple fashion. Pop open that **functions.php** file and write your first custom function:

chapter_05/v2/wicked/functions.php

```php
<?php
function wicked_footer_pagelinks() {
  echo '<ul id="simplepages">';
  wp_list_pages('depth=1&sort_column=menu_order&title_li=');
  echo '</ul>';
}
?>
```

It's fairly straightforward: we're using PHP's `echo` function to spit out a `ul` element wrapping the list of pages, with an `id` so we can target it easily in our CSS. The only tricky part is the argument string passed to `wp_list_pages`.

As always, the ultimate reference for understanding how to use a WordPress function is the Codex, but I'll break down the arguments I'm using here. *depth* specifies how far WordPress should dig into the site's page hierarchy. By specifying 1, we're telling WordPress that we only want top-level

---

[5] http://codex.wordpress.org/Template_Tags/wp_list_pages

pages. *sort_column* specifies how the pages should be sorted. There are a number of different options that can be provided here: you can sort by ID, name, author, date modified, and so on. menu_order is the way the pages are ordered by the user in the admin section, so it's a sensible choice. *title_li* is used to set a title that will appear at the top of the list. By passing in ' ' (an empty string), we're telling WordPress to omit the title, and also not to wrap the pages in a ul (since we're providing that ourselves).

Again, all these parameters (and several others) are described on the Codex page for the wp_list_pages, so you should have a read through that, or the page of any WordPress function you plan on using.

Now that we've created our function in **functions.php**, back in our footer we can call on the function like so:

chapter_05/v2/wicked/footer-homepage.php (excerpt)

```
<div id="footer">
  <?php
    wicked_footer_pagelinks();
    // action hook creating the footer
    thematic_footer();
  ?>
</div><!-- #footer -->
```

Save all your changes, jump into your browser, and head on over to your child theme's home page. If all went well, your list of pages will be waiting for you at the bottom. Now all you need to do is add some CSS to make them pretty, and you're ready to rumble! Here are some starter styles that display the items horizontally and lose those pesky bullet points:

chapter_05/v2/wicked/newstyles.css (excerpt)

```
body.home ul#simplepages {
  width: 940px;
  margin: 0 auto;
}

body.home ul#simplepages li {
  list-style-type: none;
  display: inline;
  margin-right: 30px;
}
```

What we've learned here is how to insert some new content using WordPress's template tags, and how to take advantage of WordPress's custom template includes. That's great, but there's one more big piece of the WordPress and Thematic puzzle that you'll need to master: hooks and filters.

Hooks and Filters

In the above example we put the markup generation inside a function in our **functions.php** file, but we still had to edit a template file to insert a call to that function. This works, but it turns out we can do this in an even cleaner way: WordPress exposes two different kinds of **hooks**, so called because code attached to a hook grabs on to WordPress's functionality like Velcro. We can create new functions in **functions.php**, attach them to these hooks, and have them modify parts of the theme's output without touching any template files.

Action hooks are provided for events, such as when a post is displayed or a page's footer is rendered. You'll commonly use an action hook when you want to attach a function you've written to a certain activity—for example, when WordPress displays a comment or widget.

Filter hooks allow you to pass content through a function and return it to WordPress—generally, these are used to modify text. For example, if you wanted to highlight certain words in your post's content, or append a special icon image to links, you'd use a filter hook on the content of your posts.

In both cases, you write your function, then write a simple line of code that registers your hook with WordPress. Then, when WordPress wants to display content or take some action that triggers one of those hooks, it goes looking for any functions that were registered to it, and executes them. No need to worry if this seems confusing right now: as soon as you've seen a few practical examples it will make perfect sense.

This book is far too small to explain every single hook in WordPress—there are over 1,100 of them! You'll find a list of all the actions available to you in the WordPress Codex Action Reference.[6] For filters, check out the WordPress Codex Filter Reference.[7] Another great reference is Adam R. Brown's WordPress Hooks Database,[8] which includes information on which hooks and filters were added or removed in each version of WordPress; you'll find that this information is absolutely essential if you're developing themes to be backwards-compatible with older versions of WordPress.

Wait a minute ... eleven *hundred* hooks?!

Yup, WordPress sure does provide a whole lot of hooks. It's okay—many of these hooks are about stuff like posting or pingbacks, and these are better suited to plugins. The most useful hooks for themers are the ones that relate to displaying markup and content.

Hooks are simple enough to use—write your function and then tell WordPress you intend to hook into it. Adding an action or filter hook is done with functions named `add_action` and `add_filter`, strangely enough:

---

[6] http://codex.wordpress.org/Plugin_API/Action_Reference
[7] http://codex.wordpress.org/Plugin_API/Filter_Reference
[8] http://adambrown.info/p/wp_hooks/

```
add_action($tag, $function_to_add, $priority, $accepted_args);
add_filter($tag, $function_to_add, $priority, $accepted_args);
```

The $tag parameter is where you specify the hook you want to add to; $function_to_add is the name of your function. The next two are optional, but worth knowing about: $priority is used to determine the order in which your action ought to occur, relative to other actions that might be happening on the same hook—larger numbers happen later. $accepted_args is a number that tells WordPress how many arguments your function will expect to receive.

If you decide that you want to "unhook" an action or filter from a hook, that is simple too. Call WordPress's remove_filter. It's constructed in much the same way, with one slight caveat: you can't call it directly, so you need to hook it onto WordPress's init action. init is an action hook that WordPress runs as soon as it loads. By delaying our remove_some_filter function slightly, we ensure that the action we're trying to remove has already been added; otherwise this would produce an error. Here's how you use remove_filter:

```
function remove_some_filter() {
  remove_filter(tag, function, priority, args);
}

add_action('init', 'remove_some_filter')
```

 ### What about `remove_action`?

What happened to remove_action, you wonder? It turns out that it's an alias for remove_filter: when you call remove_action, WordPress simply calls remove_filter, which can remove either action or filter hooks. If you'd rather keep your code readable by always using remove_action for hooks you know to be actions, go right ahead. If you find it simpler just to use remove_filter all the time, then feel free to do that instead. Either approach is quite correct.

 ### Get Your Priorities Straight

If an action or filter was assigned a priority when it was added, you *must* specify the *same* priority if you remove it. Otherwise WordPress won't remove it, nor give you any clues as to why not. This can be particularly frustrating if you're unaware of this rule! So remember: if remove_filter is failing, be sure to check if the hook was added with a priority.

A thoughtfully developed theme framework will also bring its own hooks to the table, each of which you can augment, remove, or replace. Thematic, of course, provides plenty—we'll talk about those in more detail later.

Adding a Favicon

Let's have a look at one simple example of how you can use a hook to modify your theme. Favicons are those little icons you see in the tabs, titles, bookmarks, and history areas of your browser. Why not add one to your theme? And while you're at it, you might like to add a larger icon for iPhones, iPads, and iPod touches.

First, create your favicon—there are plenty of online resources to help you out.[9] Call your icon **favicon.ico**, and upload it to your theme's directory.

Next, in **functions.php**, we'll make a simple function that constructs a link to the location of the favicon. The URL of your theme's files is provided by WordPress's `get_bloginfo`[10] function, and we'll specify the rest of the URL ourselves:

```
                                          chapter_05/v3/wicked/functions.php (excerpt)

function wicked_favicon() {
  echo '<link rel="shortcut icon" href="'
      . get_bloginfo('stylesheet_directory')
      . '/images/favicon.ico"/>';
}
```

Note that in the above code, we've assumed that your favicon will live in a directory called **images**—if you put them elsewhere, be sure to say so in your function.

Now, we need to add the action to the theme's `head`. Fortunately WordPress has an action hook that's triggered when the `head` element is being constructed: it's called `wp_head`. So, following the format we saw above for using `add_action`, all we need to write is:

```
                                          chapter_05/v3/wicked/functions.php (excerpt)

add_action('wp_head', 'wicked_favicon');
```

Because the order of links in the `head` is of no consequence to us, there's no need to worry about specifying a priority; our `wicked_favicon` function accepts no arguments, so it's unnecessary to specify `$accepted_args` either. That leaves us with just the action we want to hook into, and the function we want to attach.

The same technique works for including extra style sheets or JavaScript files—anything that ought to go in the `head` can be added to `wp_head`.

---

[9] http://www.sitepoint.com/blogs/2009/02/27/88-outstanding-favicons-and-6-resources-to-help-you-create-your-own/

[10] http://codex.wordpress.org/Function_Reference/get_bloginfo

Thematic's Hooks

Of course, adding markup to your theme's head element is fairly uninteresting: most times you'll want to be playing with markup inside the site's body. Fortunately, Thematic provides a number of its own hooks, which we can use to add, remove, or adjust code at varying points throughout any page. Most of them are named according to where they are in the template, or what they do; here are the hooks you'll find most useful as a themer:

- thematic_before
- thematic_aboveheader
- thematic_header—this builds the entire header div and also contains the following actions:
    - thematic_brandingopen
    - thematic_blogtitle
    - thematic_blogdescription
    - thematic_brandingclose
    - thematic_access—this builds the menu, and a "skip to content" link
- thematic_belowheader
- thematic_abovecontent
- thematic_abovepost
- thematic_belowpost
- thematic_abovecomments
- thematic_belowcomments
- thematic_abovecommentslist
- thematic_belowcommentslist
- thematic_abovetrackbackslist
- thematic_belowtrackbackslist
- thematic_abovecommentsform
- thematic_belowcommentsform
- thematic_show_subscription_checkbox
- thematic_show_manual_subscription_form
- thematic_abovemainasides—asides are what Thematic calls its widget areas
- thematic_betweenmainasides
- thematic_belowmainasides
- thematic_abovefooter
- thematic_after

If you're the more visual type, check out this nifty wireframe[11] by ThemeShaper Forums member dwenaus. It shows every widget area, major chunks of markup, and the most useful hooks as they appear in a template.

---

[11] http://bluemandala.com/thematic/thematic-structure.html

Unless you have a much better memory than me, though, you'll probably never remember every hook and function available to you, so there's no sense in trying to learn them. Instead, you should focus on learning the *process* of finding what you want. Dig into the templates and Thematic's extension files, and consult the WordPress Codex when you run into functions that are part of WordPress's core functionality. To give you an idea of how that's done, let's tackle an example from top to bottom.

Putting It All Together

Before we move onto some more sophisticated modifications of our theme, I want to show you just one example of how all those template files and hooks work together to create the markup that you see when you load the site in your browser. **single.php** is a good template to start with; it's the one that controls the display of a single post. Pop it open with your favorite text editor and take a peek:

thematic/single.php

```php
<?php

  // calling the header.php
  get_header();

  // action hook for placing content above #container
  thematic_abovecontainer();

?>

    <div id="container">

    <?php thematic_abovecontent(); ?>

    <div id="content">

      <?php

      the_post();

      // create the navigation above the content
      thematic_navigation_above();

      // calling the widget area 'single-top'
      get_sidebar('single-top');

      // action hook creating the single post
      thematic_singlepost();

      // calling the widget area 'single-insert'
      get_sidebar('single-insert');
```

```
        // create the navigation below the content
        thematic_navigation_below();

        // calling the comments template
        thematic_comments_template();

        // calling the widget area 'single-bottom'
        get_sidebar('single-bottom');

        ?>

    </div><!-- #content -->

    <?php thematic_belowcontent(); ?>

  </div><!-- #container -->
<?php

  // action hook for placing content below #container
  thematic_belowcontainer();

  // calling the standard sidebar
  thematic_sidebar();

  // calling footer.php
  get_footer();

?>
```

As we saw when we looked at **home.php** and **footer.php**, there's little in the way of actual markup in this file. If we want to find out how the post's heading, byline, and body are put together, we're going to have to dig a little deeper.

 It's a Jungle in There

Thematic's extension files are well-commented, but they're often quite long. You'll soon be making fast friends with the search function in your text editor. If it features a project-wide search function that lets you search for a string across multiple files in your working directory, it's definitely a good idea to become acquainted with it now.

If your favorite editor lacks this functionality, one alternative is to search Thematic's source code on Google Code,[12] where it's hosted. Just click on the **Source** tab, and then search for the function or hook that you're looking for. Google Code will show you every occurrence of that text across Thematic's entire codebase, complete with context and line numbers.

---

[12] http://code.google.com/p/thematic/

`thematic_singlepost` is the function that pulls in the post itself. Searching for "thematic_singlepost" across the entire **thematic** directory reveals that the function declaration lies in **library/extensions/content-extensions.php**:

thematic/library/extensions/content-extensions.php (excerpt)

```
// Located in single.php
// The Post
function thematic_singlepost() {
  do_action('thematic_singlepost');
} //end thematic_singlepost
```

`do_action` is a way to tell WordPress that an action is taking place, so it should execute any functions that are hooked to that action. This is an important concept that might be a little confusing, so let's break it down:

1. When WordPress is rendering the **single.php** template, it comes across a call to the `thematic_singlepost()` function.

2. When it runs that function, Thematic tells WordPress to trigger the `thematic_singlepost` *action*.

3. At that point, any functions that have been attached to that hook—via `add_action` as we saw above—will be executed.

So, in order to find out what exactly Thematic does next, we just need to find the functions that are hooked to that action. Let's search for the next instance of the string "thematic_singlepost," which turns out to be further down in the same file:

thematic/library/extensions/content-extensions.php (excerpt)

```
add_action('thematic_singlepost', 'thematic_single_post');
```

Aha! There's our `add_action` call. It's telling WordPress that when the event `thematic_singlepost` occurs, we want to do whatever's contained in the function `thematic_single_post` (note the extra underscore). We're getting warmer! Lucky for us, that function is located just above the `add_action` call:

thematic/library/extensions/content-extensions.php (excerpt)

```
function thematic_single_post() { ?>
<div id="post-<?php the_ID(); ?>" class="<?php thematic_post_class(); ?>">
  <?php thematic_postheader(); ?>
    <div class="entry-content">
      <?php thematic_content(); ?>
      <?php wp_link_pages('before=<div class="page-link">' .
➥__('Pages:', 'thematic') . '&after=</div>') ?>
```

```
    </div>
  <?php thematic_postfooter(); ?>
</div><!-- .post -->
<?php
}
```

Found it! Well, mostly—much of this code is still calling on other functions we've yet to discover. Some of them, like `thematic_content`, are other functions in Thematic's library. Others, like `wp_link_pages`, are built-in WordPress functionality. Despite these other function calls, however, this code bears a resemblance to what we think a post should be made of. There's a `div` with some `class`es and an `id`, a post header function, another `div` with the content inside, pagination, and a post footer function.

That sure is a lot of searching to find out how one little object works. Why, you might ask, is everything stashed away in function upon function upon function? While it might seem like a lot of fiddling about, it's actually for your benefit—breaking up all the functional elements into tiny chunks means that we can target specific parts of the template, reuse a lot of those Thematic functions in our own work, and generally have a lot of flexibility to change stuff.

Time for a Break

That was a lot of information, and we're yet to do very much actual template hacking! Rest assured, it's all important: the more you understand the WordPress theming engine, the better equipped you are to make some seriously wicked themes. As you become acquainted with WordPress and Thematic, you'll find that a good understanding of all these bits and pieces will make it easier for you to make precision changes to existing templates, or even build all-new ones.

For now, though, it's probably time to grab a snack or tasty beverage. When you return, we'll start putting that big, fat stack of knowledge to good use.

Pimping Your Child Theme

Back already? Great! We're ready to start hacking on some of those juicy templates. We'll make three more changes, in increasing order of complexity: first, we'll add social media share buttons to every post; then, we'll add author bios to the bottom of the posts; and finally, we'll finish our magazine-style home page layout with a full-width featured post and a few excerpts.

Adding a Social Media Button to Your Posts

All of the modifications we've made so far have relied on action hooks. Let's try one with a filter hook, shall we? Unlike an action, a filter will receive some content from WordPress that it can modify and must then pass along, so that lower priority filters can act on it, and so that it can be output. This means that your filter function should accept an argument (the initial content), and needs to return the modified content (the output) when it's done.

For this example, we'll be adding a social media share button to the end of every post. We'll grab a nifty combined share button from AddThis,[13] though you could use whatever share buttons or combination of them you prefer. Head on over to AddThis.com and grab yourself a button (choose **Website** from **Select your service**, as the **WordPress** option provides you with a plugin rather than a code snippet). At the end of the process, you'll be given some HTML to copy and paste into your template. We'll use that in our function:

chapter_05/v4/wicked/functions.php *(excerpt)*

```
function wicked_linklove($content) {
  if(is_single()) {
    $content .= '<div class="linklove">
      Did you love this post? Tell everyone you know, right now!
      ⋮ Paste the markup you received from AddThis here.
    </div>';
  }
  return $content;
}
```

Notice that, unlike the action hook functions we wrote previously, this one accepts an argument: `$content`. That parameter will contain whatever content WordPress is applying a filter to. We take that variable and append our new `.linklove` div to it, then return it for subsequent filters or for display (if our filter was the last one).

 Pass It Along

If you forget to return the content at the end of your filter, your filter will act like a black hole: WordPress will pass the content in, but nothing will come out. That would result in the entire contents of all our posts disappearing!

We're also using a quick `if` statement to check if the post is being displayed on its own page: we only want to display the share link on the full view, not in excerpts. This is accomplished with WordPress's `is_page` function. WordPress has a great selection of these conditional tags[14] that allow you to display content based on the conditions met by the current page; it's worth becoming familiar with them.

Now to tell WordPress to apply this filter to each post's content. Thematic passes the full content of every post through a filter handily named `thematic_post`, so let's try using that:

chapter_05/v4/wicked/functions.php *(excerpt)*

```
add_filter('thematic_post','wicked_linklove', 90);
```

---

[13] http://www.addthis.com/
[14] http://codex.wordpress.org/Conditional_Tags

We have used a priority of 90 to try to ensure that our filter will execute after any other filters modifying the same content; the priority argument is entirely relative to the other filters, so if it appears in the wrong place just try adjusting the number up or down. Load it up in your browser: instant social media rockstardom is yours!

Showing an Author Bio on a Post

Many blogs often include a small biography of the author/s at the bottom of a post. Here's how to add a bio box to the end of your posts. We'll be using the same `thematic_post` filter that we used above.

First, let's write our function—the pattern should be growing familiar to you by now! The first `if` statement checks to see if we're in a single post or a page (as we only want to display the author bio on the full view, and not in lists of posts). Assuming either of these conditions is true, our function then builds a `div`, a heading for the author's name, the author's Gravatar at a size of 50 pixels, and the bio from the author's WordPress profile. We then return the post content with the new `div` attached. Here's our function:

chapter_05/v5/wicked/functions.php (excerpt)

```php
function wicked_showbio($content)  {
  if (is_single()) {
    $content .=  '<div id="authorbio">';
    $content .= '<h3>About ' . get_the_author() . '</h3>';
    $content .= '<p>' . get_avatar(get_the_author_meta("user_email"), "50");
    $content .= get_the_author_description() .'</p></div>';
  }
  return $content;
}
```

You'll see that we've used some functions beginning with the word "get"—`get_the_author`, `get_avatar`, `get_the_author_meta`, and `get_the_author_description`. These are functions WordPress provides to retrieve author info and avatars.

Is there an echo in here?

As a general rule, WordPress functions beginning with `the_` include an `echo` statement, whereas those beginning with `get_the_` don't. For example, WordPress includes both `the_author`[15] and `get_the_author`[16] methods. Both retrieve the same information, but `get_the_author` returns it for you to use in your PHP code, whereas `the_author` outputs it directly using `echo`.

Therefore:

```php
<?php the_author ?>
```

is exactly the same as:

```php
<?php echo get_the_author ?>
```

If you tried to use `the_author` by mistake in the `wicked_showbio` function, you'd end up with a mess: PHP would output the author name as soon as you called `the_author`, which is well before you return `$content` to the filter. This would result in the author names showing up at the top of the post, instead of where you wanted them.

In **functions.php**, a filter for `thematic_post` will take care of attaching our function to the end of the post content:

chapter_05/v5/wicked/functions.php *(excerpt)*

```php
add_filter('thematic_post','wicked_showbio', '70');
```

Remember to add some CSS to your theme to make that new `div` look sexy.

Posts with Excerpts

For our last trick, we'll take some more drastic action: we'll remove the default list of posts from the front page and replace it with a list of our own making. We'll grab the four most recent posts: the newest will live in a large feature area and display its post thumbnail, with the next three arranged chronologically beneath it. Imagine a similar layout to Figure 5.1.

---

[15] http://codex.wordpress.org/Template_Tags/the_author
[16] http://codex.wordpress.org/Template_Tags/get_the_author

Figure 5.1. A big feature area

Setting Up Post Thumbnails

First, we'll need to include post thumbnail support for our theme. Post thumbnails were introduced in version 2.9 of WordPress, enabling you to attach a feature image when you create a post. Your theme can provide support for this feature, define a number of various thumbnail sizes, and use different versions of the thumbnail in various listings. For example, you might want to use a small, square-sized thumbnail for search results and archive listings, a medium square for the home page, and a large, full-width size for single posts.

To enable thumbnail support in our theme, let's add this code to **functions.php**:

(excerpt)

```
add_theme_support('post-thumbnails');
```

`set_post_thumbnail_size` is the WordPress function used to specify a default size for the image, while `add_image_size` defines other thumbnail sizes. Our home page is likely to be the only place where we'll want a square image of this size; if we want to add thumbnails to other parts of the template, such as the single post template, they'll almost certainly be a different size. So let's make the default one nice and big, and choose a medium size for the home page image:

(excerpt)

```
set_post_thumbnail_size(540, 300, true);
add_image_size('homepage-thumbnail', 300, 200, true);
```

Both of those functions accept the same three parameters: the width of the thumbnail, its height, and a Boolean option that tells WordPress whether or not to **hard crop** the images. If you set this to `false` or omit it, the images will be scaled to *fit in a box of the given dimensions* while retaining their proportions; if you set it to `true` they will be *cropped to exactly those dimensions*—a hard crop, if you like. From now on, whenever a user of the theme attaches a new featured image, WordPress will create those two sizes for us. Sorted!

Building The Loop

Our next task is to create a function to build a new Loop. As Brandon mentioned back in Chapter 2, The Loop is a process that grabs one or more posts, and it's used wherever you need post information to appear. Any code that lives inside The Loop will appear for every post in the list. You can read all about The Loop on the WordPress Codex.[17]

On a blog's home page, The Loop grabs a list of the most recent blog posts. The number of posts it retrieves for listing pages is defined in the WordPress settings, under **Reading**. We only want four posts on our home page, so if we wanted to be lazy we could ask our users to enter 4 in that field. But this is impractical; that setting would also be used for search results, category and tag pages, and monthly archives, too. Instead, we should be polite and override that behavior just for our home page.

To start with, we'll use WordPress's function for retrieving lists of posts: `query_posts`. This way we can choose what sorts of posts should appear in a list, in which order, and the amount. Our needs are simple: we just want the four most recent posts. We'll create a new function, `wicked_indexloop`, and call on `query_posts` like so:

---

[17] http://codex.wordpress.org/The_Loop

chapter_05/v6/wicked/functions.php *(excerpt)*

```
function wicked_indexloop() {
  query_posts("posts_per_page=4");
}
```

This will grab the first four posts to display on the front page. Next, we'll include the loop—excuse me, The Loop—in our function:

chapter_05/v6/wicked/functions.php *(excerpt)*

```
function wicked_indexloop() {
  query_posts("posts_per_page=4");
  if (have_posts()) : while (have_posts()) : the_post(); ?> ❶
    : we'll do some stuff here
  <?php endwhile; else: ?> ❷
    : if there are no posts, we'll display an error
  <?php endif;
  wp_reset_query(); ❸
}
```

❶ These statements check to see if we have posts; for each post, we'll display some content, though we don't need to worry about that just yet.

❷ If the query fails to find any posts, we'll display a message.

❸ Finally, we tidy up The Loop by using `wp_reset_query`, which destroys the query we started with—failing to do so could interfere with conditional tags further down the page.

The Loop Is Your New Best Friend

As you become a more accomplished themer, you'll find that `query_posts`[18] and The Loop[19] will become some of your favorite tools. When you're done playing with these examples, it's well worth your time to check out the Codex entries for each.

Advanced Querying

`query_posts` replaces the active Loop on a page. If, down the road, you find yourself wanting to display your custom Loop *in addition to* the default Loop, or if you want multiple custom Loops, you'll need to dig into the documentation for the `WP_Query`[20] class—a more flexible way of using The Loop. It's beyond the scope of what we want to do here, but you might want to become familiar with it as you become more experienced with WordPress.

---

[18] http://codex.wordpress.org/Function_Reference/query_posts
[19] http://codex.wordpress.org/The_Loop
[20] http://codex.wordpress.org/Function_Reference/WP_Query

We're now ready to start plugging in the code that will make our posts appear. Remember earlier in the chapter when we went hunting for the function `thematic_single_post`? It'd be great for our custom Loop to still have all that juicy Thematic functionality, so we'll reuse some of the functions we found there: `thematic_post_class`, which generates that big collection of classes we find on every post, and `thematic_postheader`, which builds a heading, byline, date, and edit link.

We also need to include the post's thumbnail for the first item only, so we'll use a counter to figure out which post we're up to. If the counter is at 1, we'll include the post's home page thumbnail using the WordPress template tag `the_post_thumbnail`. At the end of The Loop, we'll increment the counter by 1. Below is the first part of The Loop:

chapter_05/v6/wicked/functions.php *(excerpt)*

```
query_posts("posts_per_page=4");
$counter = 1;
if (have_posts()) : while (have_posts()) : the_post(); ?>
  <div id="post-<?php the_ID() ?>" class="<?php thematic_post_class() ?>">
    <?php thematic_postheader();
    if ($counter == 1 && has_post_thumbnail()) {
      the_post_thumbnail('homepage-thumbnail');
    } ?>
    <div class="entry-content">
      <?php the_excerpt(); ?>
      <a href="<?php the_permalink(); ?>" class="more"><?php echo more_text() ?>
➡</a>
      <?php $counter++; ?>
    </div>
  </div><!-- .post -->
<?php endwhile; else: ?>
```

The only other new function used here is `more_text`: it's a Thematic method that displays a "Read More" link that's been passed through a filter, so it's easy to modify on a site-wide basis.

Our last little task is to define a message to display if the query retrieved no posts:

chapter_05/v6/wicked/functions.php *(excerpt)*

```
<?php endwhile; else: ?>
  <h2>Eek</h2>
  <p>There are no posts to show!</p>
<?php endif;
```

Here's the entire function, put together:

chapter_05/v6/wicked/functions.php *(excerpt)*

```php
function wicked_indexloop() {
  query_posts("posts_per_page=4");
  $counter = 1;
  if (have_posts()) : while (have_posts()) : the_post(); ?>
    <div id="post-<?php the_ID() ?>" class="<?php thematic_post_class() ?>">
      <?php thematic_postheader(); ?>
      if ($counter == 1 && has_post_thumbnail() && !is_paged()) {
        the_post_thumbnail('homepage-thumbnail');
      } ?>
      <div class="entry-content">
        <?php the_excerpt(); ?>
        <a href="<?php the_permalink(); ?>" class="more">
➥<?php echo more_text() ?></a>
        <?php $counter++; ?>
      </div>
    </div><!-- .post -->
  <?php endwhile; else: ?>
    <h2>Eek</h2>
    <p>There are no posts to show!</p>
  <?php endif;
  wp_reset_query();
}
```

Inserting The Loop

Whew! With all that done, we can now insert it into the **home.php** template. Look for the line where `thematic_indexloop` is called:

```php
// action hook creating the index loop
thematic_indexloop();
```

All you need to do is replace it with a comment of your own and a call to the `wicked_indexloop` function:

chapter_05/v6/wicked/home.php *(excerpt)*

```php
// action hook creating the index loop
//thematic_indexloop();

// a custom homepage loop
wicked_indexloop();
```

Check out your blog's home page; you should now see four posts, and if the most recent one has a thumbnail attached to it, that should be sitting there too.

There's one slight problem, though: because we've replaced the default Loop with our own, the pagination links to older posts no longer work as intended. Because we're going for a magazine-style home page rather than a straight-up blog, we can simply remove those links, which are generated by the call to `thematic_navigation_below`:

chapter_05/v6/wicked/home.php *(excerpt)*

```php
// create the navigation below the content
thematic_navigation_below();
```

Remove or comment out that line, and you should be good to go!

All that's left now is to style up those four posts as you see fit: Thematic's dynamic `class`es will take care of identifying them for you, and arranging them should be a piece of cake. The following example styles will create the basic layout:

chapter_05/v6/wicked/newstyles.css *(excerpt)*

```css
body.home div.p1 {
  font-size: 120%;
}

body.home div.p1 img {
  float: left;
  margin-right: 30px;
}

body.home div.p2 {
  clear: left;
}

body.home div.p2,
body.home div.p3,
body.home div.p4 {
  width: 270px;
  float: left;
  margin-top: 22px;
}

body.home div.p3 {
  margin-left: 30px;
  margin-right: 30px;
}
```

Red-hot Tips for Themers

As we've progressed through this chapter, you've seen three different ways to modify your child theme: by creating and modifying template files, by using WordPress's file include functionality, or by hooking into actions and filters in your **functions.php** file. We've also seen quite a few examples of how to bend WordPress and Thematic to your will using those three techniques.

I want to close off this chapter with a few hints and tips that will help you be the best themer you can be.

Comments, Comments, Comments!

Have you ever found yourself lost in a maze of unfamiliar code, looking for a sign—any sign—of what it does and why it's there? Worse yet, has it been code you've written yourself? Sure, right now you might know your code backwards and forwards, but what about in three or six months' time when you want to update it? And what if you're releasing your theme to the public?

Save yourself, and your users, some aggravation by leaving copious comments in your code. Bits are free!

A Place for Everything, and Everything in Its Place

If you have more than a few custom functions in your **functions.php** file, it's probably time to start organizing them into separate files.

For example, you might want to move all your content filters into their own file. To do so, grab them out of your functions file and paste them into a new one—let's call it **functions-contentfilters.php**. For extra neatness, create a new subdirectory in your theme's directory, and give it a useful name—say, **library**.

Next, in your **functions.php** file, include it like so:

```
include('library/functions-contentfilters.php');
```

Separating your functions by purpose means that you, and your theme's users, will find it super-easy to locate your handiwork later on.

A Case of Mistaken Identities

Remember, your theme will form just one part of a website. WordPress, plugins, and your theme all work together. If any of your functions' names clash with one from a plugin or WordPress itself, there'll be confusion—and bugs—aplenty. It's a good idea to prefix all your function names with a reasonably unique string—the prevailing best practice in the WordPress community is to use an abbreviated form of your theme's name, as we've done with our Wicked theme throughout the chapter.

What's in a name?

It might be tempting to start all your function names with `wp` (for WordPress) or `theme` (because it is one, right?), but strings like these are often in use by WordPress and may well cause conflicts. Seriously, stick with the name.

Keep On Exploring

In this chapter, we learned how to override Thematic's templates with code of our own making: we looked at how to create an all-new home page for our child theme with just a little poking and prodding, and how to add new features with hooks and filters.

What we've seen here is only a taster of what's possible: it's time for you to go out there, explore, and come up with some wicked new ways to enhance your theme.

By the way, many of the skills you pick up when adding functions to your theme will stand you in good stead if you ever plan to become a plugin developer: the methodology is much the same. Bonus!

Widgets

by Allan Cole

When you're making changes to your template's code, as we did in the last chapter, it's always worth asking yourself if you can implement your change as a new widget area, or as a custom widget. For example, in the last chapter, we saw how to add a list of pages to the site's footer. Why not just add a new widget area to the site's footer, and create a custom widget for displaying only top-level pages? That way users could display the list of pages there if they wanted to, but could also choose to display nothing, or to display entirely different content.

In this chapter you'll learn how to customize your theme by adding widget-ready areas, and how to create your own custom widgets to package with your theme.

Understanding Widgets and Widget-ready Areas

Brandon told you quite a bit about widgets while you were learning to plan and design your theme, but now's a good time for a quick review. Widgets allow users to insert all sorts of content into many different site areas with ease. If the user would like to display a list of the site's categories in the sidebar, then all they need to do is drag the Categories widget onto one of the sidebar widget areas, and voilà! Instant gratification. WordPress includes about a dozen different widgets by default, but plugins and themes can add new ones, so in reality there's no limit to the number and variety of widgets users of your theme will have access to.

Before your users can take advantage of the functionality that widgets offer, you need to provide them with a place to put those widgets in your theme. Within a standard WordPress theme, you'll find at least one **widget-ready area** (alternatively referred to as a sidebar or an aside). Widget-ready areas come in all shapes and sizes depending on the theme, but they all serve the same function: they're empty containers into which WordPress users can place widgets. In fact, WordPress.org requires that every theme in its directory have at least one widget-ready area.

Many theme developers refer to these widget-ready areas as sidebars. For many designers the idea of a sidebar implies a traditional two-column blog layout, but widgets can really be used anywhere, giving your users access to this powerful functionality anywhere within the theme. Common examples of widgetized areas include leaderboards, inline ad spaces, and additional footer contents.

The Thematic theme framework uses the term **asides** to describe its widget-ready areas, which is actually very appropriate when you think about it. Thematic boasts 13 of these asides to give you detailed control over the design and layout of your site.

Default Widgets

To avoid recreating functionality that already exists, let's have a look at the default widgets available in WordPress out of the box:

Archives
> displays links to monthly archives of all the site's posts

Calendar
> displays a calendar to allow visitors to navigate through previous posts

Categories
> a list or drop-down showing the site's categories; they can be displayed either aligned or as a nested hierarchy, and you can also optionally display post counts in each one

Custom Menu
> available only from WordPress 3.0 onwards, this allows users to display one of their custom menus in a widget-ready area

Links
> this presents a list of links (for example, a blogroll)

Meta
> the login and logout links for the site

Pages
> a list of the site's pages

Recent Posts
> lists the most recent posts

Recent Comments

the most recent comments on the site

RSS

this is used to display entries from any RSS or Atom feed; it can be entries from another blog, or updates from any service that provides an RSS feed

RSS Links

links to the site's primary RSS feed and its comment RSS feed

Tag Cloud

displays the site's tags, with their font size determined by the number of posts they're attached to

Text

the most versatile widget, allowing users to insert arbitrary text or HTML (for example, it can be used to display a video from a third-party site that provides embed codes, an advertisement, or a short mission statement)

Search

the site's search form

Thematic's Widget-ready Areas

Before you go merrily adding widget areas to your child theme, it's worth having a look at Thematic's existing asides to see if one of them might serve your purpose.

I'm sure you'll find they're fairly self-explanatory:

Primary Aside

one of two main asides, which comes right after the content container in the markup on all pages, and which is commonly displayed as a sidebar

Secondary Aside

the other main aside, which comes after the primary aside and is also usually shown as a sidebar

Subsidiary Asides (3)

three widget-ready areas that appear in the footer

Index Top

an aside that appears at the top of the index page

Index Insert

this area's inserted after a certain number of posts on the index page; the number can be set in Thematic's options page in the WordPress admin section

Index Bottom

    an area that appears at the bottom of the index page

Single Top

    a widget area that appears at the top of a single-post page

Single Insert

    a widget area that presents on a single post page, between the post content and the comments

Single Bottom

    this area appears at the bottom of single post pages

Page Top

    a widget area that is inserted at the top of page templates

Page Bottom

    A widget area that's placed at the bottom of page templates

All of these asides have Thematic's usual abundance of `class` attributes, so they're dead simple to move around and style with CSS.

Widget Markup

Soon we'll be learning how to add a new widget-ready area to our theme, but first let's have a look at the sort of markup that an active widget will generate. WordPress outputs the widget-ready area as an unordered list, with a list item for each widget the area contains. In addition, when using Thematic, each widget area will be wrapped in a `div` with a `class` of `aside` and an `id` corresponding to the widget's ID (we'll see how that's set shortly).

Here's the markup for Thematic's Primary Aside:

```
<div id="primary" class="aside main-aside">
  <ul class="xoxo">
    <li id="linkcat-2" class="widgetcontainer widget_links">
      <h3 class="widgettitle">Blogroll</h3>
      <ul class="xoxo blogroll">
        <li><a href="#">Link #1</a></li>
        <li><a href="#">Link #2</a></li>
        <li><a href="#">Link #3</a></li>
      </ul>
    </li>
  </ul><!-- END #xoxo -->
</div><!-- END #first -->
```

The highlighted area here represents the actual widget being used—in this example it's WordPress's built-in Links widget. Thematic has filters that allow you to modify the markup elements that make up widgets and widget-ready areas:

thematic_before_widget_area

the opening <div> tag

thematic_after_widget_area

the closing </div> tag

thematic_before_widget

the opening <li> tag before each widget; the default value is:

```
<li id="%1$s" class="widgetcontainer %2$s">
```

Those odd-looking %1$s and %2$s bits allow WordPress to generate a numbered id and a class for each widget that's added, like linkcat-2 and widget_links in the previous code example.

thematic_after_widget

the closing </li> tag

thematic_before_title

the opening h3 tag before each widget's title

thematic_after_title

the closing h3 tag after each widget's title

Let's look at a quick example of putting these filters to use. Let's say you wanted the widget titles to be wrapped in h4 elements instead of h3s. Easy:

chapter_06/v1/wicked/functions.php (excerpt)

```
function wicked_before_title($content) {
  $content = '<h4 class="widgettitle">';
  return $content;
}
function wicked_after_title($content) {
  $content = '</h4>';
  return $content;
}
add_filter('thematic_before_title', 'wicked_before_title');
add_filter('thematic_after_title', 'wicked_after_title');
```

This is a little different from the way we used filters in the last chapter: instead of modifying the $content variable, we're flat-out overwriting it. This might seem odd, but it's perfectly okay, and it's nice and simple.

Adding a Custom Widget-ready Area to Your Theme

We've seen that Thematic includes three widget-ready areas in the footer, called subsidiary asides. All three are wrapped in a container div with an id of subsidiary.

For our example, we'll add another widget area above that container, which can be styled to be full-width, to replace the hardcoded page list we added in Chapter 5.

Registering a Widget-ready Area

The first step in adding a new widget-ready area to your theme is to register it with WordPress, so that it will appear in the widget administration interface.

To keep our **functions.php** file nice and tidy, let's create a new file in the **library** directory of our child theme; we'll call it **widget-areas.php** and include it as follows in **functions.php**:

chapter_06/v2/wicked/functions.php *(excerpt)*

```
include('library/widget-areas.php');
```

In this file, we'll put all the code required to register and display our new widget-ready area. To register it we need to call on WordPress's register_sidebar function. It accepts an array of options that define the new sidebar:

chapter_06/v2/wicked/library/widget-areas.php *(excerpt)*

```php
<?php

// Register the extra Footer Aside
function wicked_footer_aside() {
  register_sidebar(array(
    'name' => 'Main Footer Aside',
    'id' => 'footer-aside',
    'description' => __('A widget area in the footer, above the subsidiary
➥asides.', 'thematic'),
    'before_widget' => thematic_before_widget(),
    'after_widget' => thematic_after_widget(),
    'before_title' => thematic_before_title(),
    'after_title' => thematic_after_title(), )
  );
}
add_action('init', 'wicked_footer_aside');

?>
```

The array passed to `register_sidebar` needs to have the following values:

name

The name of the widget that shows up in the back end. The name is also used in the CSS `class` that I mentioned earlier. We're calling our new widget-ready area "Main Footer Aside."

id

This is used to set an ID for WordPress's sake, which you'll need to use when you're adding the widget-ready area to your templates. It's also used on the front end as the `div` element's `id`. We're using `footer-aside` here.

description

As the name suggests, this should describe the intended use or location of the sidebar. It's only shown in the back-end interface. Our description is "A widget-ready area in the footer, above the subsidiary asides." For details on that funky-looking __() code, seethe note titled Localization below.

before_widget, after_widget, before_title, and after_title

This is where you'll specify the markup that will be inserted before and after each widget and widget title. Fortunately, Thematic already has functions to generate this markup for you, which pass the content through the filters we saw earlier. If you need your aside to have different markup from the other widget-ready areas, you can change it here; for now we'll use Thematic's functions so that they'll be consistent with other widget-ready areas in the theme.

 Localization

The __() function used in the above example is a translation function. When writing themes or plugins for distribution, it's best practice to run any text through this function, so that it can be easily translated by your end users. Rather than digging through your PHP files to translate your theme's text, they can simply upload a translation file that includes localized variants of every message your theme uses. When WordPress encounters the __() method, it will go looking for a translation of that message in the user's chosen language. If it finds one, it will substitute it. The extra '*thematic*' parameter passed to the functions is what's called a domain; it's used in a situation where the same message might need to be translated differently in alternative contexts.

There's no pressure to fully understand WordPress localization; just remember to wrap any text in your theme's interface in the translation function, and you'll be doing your job.

For more info about how to use `register_sidebar`, you guessed it: check out the WordPress Codex.[1]

---

[1] http://codex.wordpress.org/Function_Reference/register_sidebar

Now that the widget-ready area is registered, it will appear in the back-end interface and you can add widgets to it. However, we've yet to call on it in any of our templates, so as they stand, these widgets would never be displayed. Let's fix that now.

Displaying a Widget-ready Area

So we've registered our new widget-ready area, but currently it only exists on the back-end interface, and nowhere on the front end. We now need to insert it in a template for it to appear. When we added the page list to the **footer-homepage.php** template in Chapter 5, we put it right above the call to thematic_footer. Now that we know about hooks, we can just add our function to that action hook and we should be good to go. Add this code to your **widget-areas.php** file:

chapter_06/v2/wicked/library/widget-areas.php (excerpt)

```
// Add footer Sidebar Area
function add_wicked_footer_aside() {
  if (is_sidebar_active('footer-aside')) {
    echo thematic_before_widget_area('footer-aside'); ❶
    dynamic_sidebar('footer-aside'); ❷
    echo thematic_after_widget_area('footer-aside'); ❸
  }
}

add_action('thematic_footer','add_wicked_footer_aside', 10);
```

What we've done here is created a function called add_wicked_footer_aside, and used it to grab our newly registered sidebar, called footer-aside, and add it to the top of Thematic's footer. There's a conditional statement—if (is_sidebar_active('footer-aside'))—that checks to see if the sidebar is active; in other words, if it has widgets added to it. This tells the theme to only show the widget area if the user has added widgets. After that come the three essential lines that we use to output the actual markup of our widget-ready area:

❶ This adds the opening markup for the widget-ready area; by default, this is a div element, though it can be modified using the thematic_before_widget_area filter we saw earlier.

❷ This is the WordPress function that displays all the widgets contained in the sidebar. You just pass in the sidebar's ID, and WordPress handles the rest.

❸ This outputs the closing markup for the widget-ready area. As above, you can filter it with thematic_after_widget_area. If you filter one, you should also filter the other to make sure the HTML tags will be matched up.

Any time you want to output a widget-ready area with the benefit of Thematic's extra markup and filters, you'll need to use those same three lines of code, so remember them well.

At this point, if you add a few widgets to your new Main Footer Aside, you should see them appear on the site above the subsidiary asides. The aside just needs a few quick styles to set it to be the same width as the main content area:

chapter_06/v2/wicked/newstyles.css *(excerpt)*

```css
#footer-aside {
  width: 940px;
  margin: 0 auto;
}
```

Victory!

Removing Widget-ready Areas

When developing your theme, it's always good to keep in mind how the publisher will use it. The 13 widget-ready areas built into Thematic really allow you to push the envelope when it comes to displaying targeted content. However, depending on your design, you may only need one or two sidebars. Especially when dealing with end-users that are new to WordPress, you want to keep the experience of administering the theme as simple as possible.

If you're designing a theme built on Thematic and you have no specific use or plans for a given widget area, you should remove it. In doing so, the back-end interface is kept cleaner, making it more organized and potentially less confusing for yourself and anyone who may use your theme. This is very easy to do with a few quick lines of code.

As an example, let's remove one of Thematic's built-in widget areas. In the last chapter, we replaced the standard Loop on the home page with a custom Loop of our own making. One consequence of this is that the `index-insert` widget area is no longer present in the template. As a result, it should be removed to prevent users being confused; at present, any widgets added to it will fail to display anywhere.

To remove the area, we need simply call on WordPress's `unregister_sidebar` method. We're adding it to the `init` hook with a priority of 20, because we want to make sure that it runs after the `register_sidebar` call that adds the sidebar in the first place:

chapter_06/v3/wicked/functions.php *(excerpt)*

```php
// remove index insert aside
function wicked_remove_index_insert() {
  unregister_sidebar('index-insert');
}
add_action('init', 'wicked_remove_index_insert', 20);
```

And that's it! If you refresh the widget admin page now, the `index-insert` box will have vanished.

Adding Custom Widgets

There are tons of plugins and widgets in the WordPress plugin directory; however, at some point you'll need to come up with your own custom widget that solves a particular problem. It's a really great selling point to have themes that come with built-in widgets, especially when they take advantage of a particular feature only available to your theme.

Traditionally, there were two ways to add your own custom widgets. The first was to simply add a function to your **functions.php** file, which is what we've been doing so far for the custom functionality of our theme. This will become quite cumbersome quickly, though with good commenting and file separation it can stay manageable. The second way of going about it is to create a WordPress plugin for each new widget. This tends to be problematic as well, because the plugin will exist separately from your theme, thereby adding a few extra administrative steps to the installation process. You want your theme to be as easy as possible to use, so this is probably best avoided.

Luckily, Thematic comes with a rather innovative built-in widget solution that makes widget creation and management extremely simple. There's a core Thematic function that looks for a folder called **widgets** in your child theme folder, and adds any widgets in there without any additional work on your part. This feature also means that your widgets will travel with your child theme, so if you're creating theme-specific widgets for distribution, you'll make things simpler for users by removing any extra plugin installation/activation steps. Another great aspect of using the **widgets** folder is that you can create each widget as a separate PHP file, which can help you stay organized.

In Chapter 5 we wrote a function to add author information to the end of every post. To make this functionality a little more flexible, why not turn it into a widget that will only display on single post pages? That way, your users can choose to display it in the sidebar, or elsewhere, or not at all.

 OOP(s)

The code that follows makes use of PHP's object oriented programming (OOP) features. If you're unfamiliar with object oriented programming, don't worry: I'll explain everything as simply as possible. This is just a warning that some of this code may seem a little strange to you if you've only ever worked with PHP in a procedural (or not object oriented) way.

Introducing the Widgets API

To create a new widget in WordPress, you extend the `WP_Widget` class. If this seems a bit beyond your grasp, don't worry: when developing WordPress widgets, it's unnecessary to think about objects and classes very much. Every widget class has the same four functions inside it, so you only need to write those four functions for every widget—and you can just copy and paste the basic layout of the class every time you want to make a new widget. The four functions you need are a constructor function (which always has the same name as the class itself), `widget`, `update`, and `form`.

Let's first have a look at the empty shell of a new widget:

```
class My_Widget extends WP_Widget {
  function My_Widget() {
    // this is a constructor, where each new instance of your widget gets built
  }

  function form($instance) {
    // this generates the widget options form which you see
    // in the widgets section in the admin
  }

  function update($new_instance, $old_instance) {
    // this handles the submission of the options form to
    // update the widget options
  }

  function widget($args, $instance) {
    // the most important function: this one handles actually outputting
    // the widget's content to the theme
  }
}
```

Assuming you've filled out each of these functions with your desired functionality, there's only one step left. Much like widget-ready areas, new widgets need to be registered with WordPress:

```
register_widget('My_Widget');
```

At the most basic level, the form and update functions only need to give your users the option to input the title to be displayed with the widget. This means that unless you require more detailed options here, you can reuse the same code for those two functions for each widget you develop.

Creating the Widget

To create our first custom widget, we'll first create a **widgets** folder inside our child theme folder, and add a new PHP file to it. We'll call it **author-data.php**. Let's start by putting in the declaration of the Author_Data_Widget class, along with the four required functions and the register_widget call:

```
                              chapter_06/v4/wicked/widgets/author-data.php (excerpt)

<?php

class Author_Data_Widget extends WP_Widget {
  function Author_Data_Widget() {

  }
```

```php
    function form($instance) {

    }

    function update($new_instance, $old_instance) {

    }

    function widget($args, $instance) {

    }
}

register_widget('Author_Data_Widget');

?>
```

Our first task is to write the constructor function. In its most basic form, it consists of:

```php
function My_Widget() {
  $this->WP_Widget($id, $name, $widget_ops, $control_ops);
}
```

That one function (`$this->WP_Widget`) is what WordPress uses to create each instance of your widget, so that's all that's necessary here. The `$id` parameter is used internally to refer to your widget, and `$name` is the name that's shown in the widget admin interface. The `$widget_ops` parameter is an array that includes the widget's description to be shown in the admin section. `$control_ops` is optional and not required for most widgets, so you can forget about it for now.

Let's have a go at writing this function for our author data widget:

chapter_06/v4/wicked/widgets/author-data.php *(excerpt)*

```php
function Author_Data_Widget() {
  $widget_ops = array(
    'description' => 'A widget that displays author info on single posts.'
  );
  $this->WP_Widget('author_data', 'Author Data', $widget_ops);
}
```

Even with only this one function in place, we can already see our widget in the back-end interface, as shown in Figure 6.1.

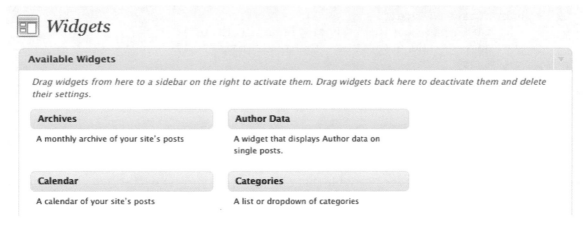

Figure 6.1. Our custom widget, as it appears in WordPress's admin section

However, if you drag the widget onto one of your widget-ready areas, you'll see that it lacks any customizable options, as shown in Figure 6.2.

Figure 6.2. Our newly defined widget has no options

We'd like our users to at least be able to set a custom title for the widget, so we should fill out the `form` and `update` functions to give us an options form. Let's start with the `form` method.

Fortunately, WordPress handles the creation of the `form` element; all you need to do is write the `label` and `input` elements specific to your option. These must be assigned specific `id` and `name` attributes in order to work correctly, but again WordPress has your back: your widget has functions called `get_field_id` and `get_field_name` that serve this purpose. Here's what our simple form looks like:

```
                                   chapter_06/v4/wicked/widgets/author-data.php (excerpt)
function form($instance) {
  $title = esc_attr($instance['title']);

  ?>
    <p>
      <label for="<?php echo $this->get_field_id('title'); ?>">Title:
```

```
      <input class="widefat"
             id="<?php echo $this->get_field_id('title'); ?>"
             name="<?php echo $this->get_field_name('title'); ?>"
             type="text"
             value="<?php echo attribute_escape($title); ?>" />
      </label>
    </p>
  <?php
}
```

The function receives an `$instance` variable that represents the current widget, which will include the options that are currently set. So, to make sure the form displays the current value of the title, we first extract the `$title` variable from `$instance`.

Then we construct the form field, using `$this->get_field_id` and `$this->get_field_name` to set the field's `id` and `name` attributes. Other than that, this is fairly straightforward HTML. If you want your form to have more than one field, all you have to do is add them here, setting their attributes appropriately.

When the form is submitted, WordPress will use your `update` function to save the options the user has entered. Let's have a look at that next:

chapter_06/v4/wicked/widgets/author-data.php *(excerpt)*

```
function update($new_instance, $old_instance) {
  $instance = $old_instance;
  $instance['title'] = strip_tags($new_instance['title']);

  return $instance;
}
```

The `update` function works a little differently: it receives two parameters, which hold a brand new widget containing the new options submitted in the form, and the old widget with the previous options, respectively. So we need to grab the title from `$new_instance`—being careful to strip out any HTML and PHP tags—and use that to set the title on our instance. To avoid confusion, we've dumped `$old_instance` into a new variable simply called `$instance`, and that's where we set the new title. Then we return `$instance`, and WordPress handles the rest, updating the widget with the options we've set.

If your form has more than one field, just repeat this process for each option that requires setting. You can include as much logic as you want in `update`. If ever you'd like to discard the new options (based on some condition), all you have to do is return `false` and the widget won't be updated.

Now that we have our options form, test it out: go back to your widgets admin page, and drag the Author Data widget onto one of the widget areas. You should see your new title form, as shown in Figure 6.3.

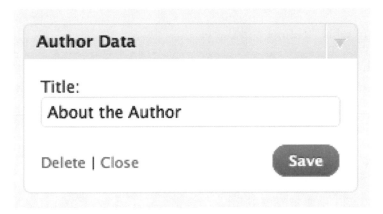

Figure 6.3. A simple widget options form

That's three out of four functions defined: we have our constructor, as well as the `form` and `update` methods for handling our widget options form. Now all that's to be done is tell WordPress how to display the widget!

Here's what that function will look like:

```
                                              chapter_06/v4/wicked/widgets/author-data.php (excerpt)
function widget($args, $instance) {
  extract($args, EXTR_SKIP); ❶

  if (is_single()) { ❷

    echo $before_widget; ❸
    $title = apply_filters('widget_title', $instance['title']); ❹

    if ( !empty( $title ) ) { echo $before_title . $title . $after_title; }; ❺
    echo '<div class="author-data">';
    echo get_avatar(get_the_author_meta('user_email'), 150); ❻
    echo '<h4>' . the_author_meta('display_name') . '</h4>';
    // Is there an author description?
    if (get_the_author_meta('description')) {
      echo '<div class="description"><p>'
          . get_the_author_meta('description')
          . '</p></div>';
    }
    echo '</div>';
    echo $after_widget; ❼
  }
}
```

Your function receives two parameters: the first one is `$args`, which is an array of the arguments provided to all widgets in your theme. They will be familiar to you: `before_title`, `after_title`, `before_widget`, and `after_widget`. The second parameter is our old friend `$instance`, which contains all the options set on your widget. In our case that's only the title.

Here's a breakdown of what's going on in there:

① First, we're using PHP's handy `extract`[2] function to break up the `$args` array into individual variables. So, from now on, instead of typing `$args['before_title']`, we can just use `$before_title`. Feel free to copy and paste this line into all your own widgets, or remove it if you prefer the more explicit `$args['before_title']` style.

② We only want to display our widget on single post pages: that's really the only place where it makes sense!

③ We echo out the standard `before_widget` string: if you've been following along with the rest of this chapter, you'll have guessed this should be Thematic's standard opening `<div>` tag.

④ We pass the title provided by the user (`$instance['title']`) through any filters applied to `widget_title` by our theme or any plugins.

⑤ As long as the title has content in it, we'll output it as well as the `$before_title` and `$after_title` values.

⑥ We use the `get_the_author_meta`[3] function a few times to grab the information we want to display about the author. In this case, we're retrieving the author's email to pass into `get_avatar`.

⑦ Finally, we output the `after_widget` value.

Now that you've written all the functions required for your widget, it should correctly display the author info on single-post pages. Give it a try!

Here's the full **author-data.php** file:

```
chapter_06/v4/wicked/widgets/author-data.php (excerpt)

<?php

class Author_Data_Widget extends WP_Widget {
  function Author_Data_Widget() {
    $widget_ops = array(
      'description' => 'A widget that displays author info on single posts.'
```

---

[2] http://php.net/manual/en/function.extract.php
[3] http://codex.wordpress.org/Function_Reference/get_the_author_meta

```php
    );
    $this->WP_Widget('author_data', 'Author Data', $widget_ops);
  }

  function form($instance) {
    $title = esc_attr($instance['title']);
    ?>
      <p>
        <label for="<?php echo $this->get_field_id('title'); ?>">Title:
        <input class="widefat"
               id="<?php echo $this->get_field_id('title'); ?>"
               name="<?php echo $this->get_field_name('title'); ?>"
               type="text"
               value="<?php echo attribute_escape($title); ?>" />
        </label>
      </p>
    <?php
  }

  function update($new_instance, $old_instance) {
    $instance = $old_instance;
    $instance['title'] = strip_tags($new_instance['title']);

    return $instance;
  }

  function widget($args, $instance) {
    extract($args, EXTR_SKIP);

    if (is_single()) {

      echo $before_widget;
      $title = apply_filters('widget_title', $instance['title']);

      if (!empty($title)) { echo $before_title . $title . $after_title; };
      echo '<div class="author-data">';
      echo get_avatar(get_the_author_meta('user_email'), 150);
      echo '<h4>' . the_author_meta('display_name') . '</h4>';

      // Is there an author description?
      if (get_the_author_meta('description')) {
        echo '<div class="description"><p>'
            . get_the_author_meta('description')
            . '</p></div>';
      }
      echo '</div>';
      echo $after_widget;
    }
  }
}
```

```
register_widget('Author_Data_Widget');

?>
```

Summary

A theme that is well-prepared with carefully placed widget-ready areas, and which takes advantage of custom widgets where appropriate to highlight its features, will often be able to outshine its competitors. We've seen fairly simple examples of the kinds of widgets you can create, but there's really no limit to what you can do: let your imagination go wild.

Here are a few final tips:

- Try not limit the functionality of your theme designs by only thinking of widget-ready areas as sidebars. Widgetized areas can be used anywhere in your site design where you think your users might want to display custom bits of content.

- Take advantage of the helpers that Thematic and WordPress provide. There's no need to reinvent the wheel when it comes to markup or hooks and filters when building widget-ready areas or custom widgets.

- Keep the back end simple for yourself, your users, or your clients by removing unnecessary clutter that's extraneous to your theme: if you haven't used or adequately styled a certain widgetized area, unregister it.

Stick to the ideas outlined here and you'll be a widget master before you know it!

Theme Options

by Allan Cole

When you start distributing your theme, within a week of release it's likely you'll receive an email like this: "Hi, I absolutely love your theme! The attention to detail and color is simply astonishing. I have one question though: how do I change X?" Initially, you might be a little annoyed. You'll be tempted to ask yourself: if this user thinks my theme is so great, why do they want to change it? The answer is simple—individuality.

Every person, and every business, is different. It's entirely natural then that a website should reflect the owner's personality and style. In this chapter, we'll look at a number of ways of making your theme as customizable as possible, so that those users won't have to resort to editing your preciously crafted template files—and you can dodge this potential support nightmare.

As Jeffrey will tell you in Chapter 8, options may be the single most important selling point for a theme. After all, if you had the choice between two themes for your business, but one of them promised the ability to customize the colors, fonts, and layout, which would you choose?

Creating an Options Panel

Before we create an options panel, we should establish what parts of our theme we'd like our users to have control over. For the purposes of illustration, I've picked the following three:

Link color
> a simple text field that allows users to define the color of links in the theme's body text, using the standard hexadecimal format (for example, #FF3366)

Custom header image

a checkbox that will add or remove a custom header background to our theme

Featured category

a drop-down select menu that lets users choose one of their site's categories; the most recent posts from that category will be used to fill out the featured post spots on the front page

As well as being the most common types of custom options you might want to add in your theme, these illustrate three different kinds of form element. Looking over these three examples in depth should give you all the knowledge you'll need to develop any type of custom option you can think of.

The good news is that there's no need to worry about reading from or writing to the WordPress database. The WordPress developers have already considered that theme and plugin developers might want to allow their users to have access to specific settings, so they've provided a trio of methods to help you out: `update_option`, `get_option`, and `delete_option`. The first adds a custom setting to the database, the second retrieves it, and the third—unsurprisingly—deletes it.

Combined with a bit of code for generating and handling the settings form itself, these three methods will allow us to develop a full-featured settings form for our theme.

Laying the Groundwork

To start off, we'll first create a new file in our **library** directory called **options.php**. This is where our custom options form and related functions will live. Before doing anything else, let's include it in **functions.php**:

chapter_07/v1/wicked/functions.php (excerpt)

```php
// include theme options
include('library/options.php');
```

We'll begin by setting a few theme-specific variables that we'll refer to later on. This is primarily to make it easier for you to adapt the code to your own theme:

chapter_07/v1/wicked/library/options.php (excerpt)

```php
<?php

// Set some theme specific variables for the options panel
$childthemename = "Wicked Theme";
$childshortname = "wt";
$childoptions = array();
```

`$childthemename` is, of course, your theme's name. We'll use this variable any time we want to display the theme's name in a link or on a page in the admin panel. Because it's a name, and will be the same in every language, no localization function is required.

`$childshortname` is an abbreviated version of your theme's name. We'll use this so that none of the settings or data we store conflicts with any other similarly named options created by WordPress, or any plugins that may be in use. We'll append it to variables like `$shortname . "_text_color"`.

`$childoptions` is where the options themselves will be stored. For the moment it's an empty array, but we'll be filling it up shortly.

Next we're going to create a function called `childtheme_options`, which will define our options and how they'll be displayed in the back-end administration interface. Inside that function we have two tasks to accomplish: we'll pull in our variables using the global keyword, and then we'll fill up the `$childoptions` array with all the information required for our options.

Let's start with the easier task:

chapter_07/v1/wicked/library/options.php *(excerpt)*

```php
function childtheme_options() {
  global $childthemename, $childshortname, $childoptions;
```

Good! Now we have access to our variables.

 Out of Range

The concept of variable scope in PHP is beyond the, uh, scope of this book. Since this is the only place we'll be using it, just include that line in your function and you'll be fine.

Next we need to define all our options. `$childoptions` is an array that contains a bunch of other arrays: one for each option you want your theme to have. Each of those arrays, in turn, should have the following values in it:

name

the name of the option

desc

holds the description of the option along with any instructions for using it; the name and description will both be displayed on your options panel

id

used to save and update the option in the database; we'll use the `$childshortname` variable here so that our field will be unique

std

> holds the default setting of the option; our form will also have a reset button, which will allow users to restore all options to the value we declare here

type

> defines the type of form element you intend to use; you can choose between text, select, textarea, radio, and checkbox

options (only for `select` and `radio` types)

> an array of the options that users will be able to choose from in select and radio button lists

Let's start with the link color option:

```
                                    chapter_07/v1/wicked/library/options.php (excerpt)

function childtheme_options() {

  ⋮

  $childoptions = array (

    array("name" => __('Link Color','thematic'),
          "desc" => __('Change the color of links by entering a HEX
➥color number. (e.g.: 003333)','thematic'),
          "id" => "wicked_link_color",
          "std" => "999999",
          "type" => "text"),

    ⋮

  );
}
```

This is fairly straightforward, right? We're using the __() localization function around the name and description, and setting a unique id. Because we need the user to enter a value, we're setting type to text: this will output a text box.

The array for the header image checkbox will be very similar, but the featured category select box is trickier: we need to provide an options value that will contain all the different categories on the site. Obviously these will vary from one site to another, so we need to retrieve them from WordPress. Fortunately there's a `get_categories`[1] method to do just that:

---

[1] http://codex.wordpress.org/Function_Reference/get_categories

```
                                chapter_07/v1/wicked/library/options.php (excerpt)

function childtheme_options() {

  ⋮

  // Create array to store the Categories to be used in the drop-down select box
  $categories_obj = get_categories('hide_empty=0');
  $categories = array();
  foreach ($categories_obj as $cat) {
    $categories[$cat->cat_ID] = $cat->cat_name;
  }

  $childoptions = array (

  ⋮

}
```

get_categories returns the categories as an array with several different values describing each category. In order to populate our select box we're going to want an array of category IDs and names, so we use a quick foreach loop to grab them.

Now that we have an array of categories, we can use it in our $childoptions array; we'll also add the checkbox while we're at it:

```
                                chapter_07/v1/wicked/library/options.php (excerpt)

function childtheme_options() {

  global $childthemename, $childshortname, $childoptions;

  // Create array to store the Categories to be used in the drop-down select box
  $categories_obj = get_categories('hide_empty=0');
  $categories = array();
  foreach ($categories_obj as $cat) {
    $categories[$cat->cat_ID] = $cat->cat_name;
  }

  $childoptions = array (

    array("name" => __('Link Color','thematic'),
          "desc" => __('Change the color of links by entering a HEX
➥color number. (e.g.: 003333)','thematic'),
          "id" => "wicked_link_color",
          "std" => "999999",
          "type" => "text"
    ),
    array( "name" => __('Show Header Image','thematic'),
          "desc" => __('Show an image in the header. Replace the header.png file
```

```
➥found in the /wicked/images/ folder with your own image.','thematic'),
          "id" => "wicked_show_logo",
          "std" => "false",
          "type" => "checkbox"
    ),
    array( "name" => __('Featured Category','thematic'),
          "desc" => __('A category of posts to be featured on the front page.',
➥'thematic'),
          "id" => "wicked_feature_cat",
          "std" => $default_cat,
          "type" => "select",
          "options" => $categories
    )
  );
}
```

After you've defined all your options, you'll need to hook this function into the WordPress `init` action. By doing this, we make sure our settings are defined after WordPress loads, but before any headers or other processes that rely on our settings are loaded. This one should be familiar to you by now:

chapter_07/v1/wicked/library/options.php (excerpt)

```
add_action('init', 'childtheme_options');
```

Adding an Admin Panel

Now that our options are defined, there are still two more steps to work through before we'll have a working options page. First, we need to add a page to the WordPress admin menu to contain our settings form. After that, we'll create a function to output the form itself.

First, the new menu item. This part of the process is the same for any options page you create, so I will avoid going into too much detail; you can simply reuse it with a few slight modifications, assuming you're using the same `$childthemename`, `$childshortname`, and `$childoptions` variables we've been using so far:

chapter_07/v1/wicked/library/options.php (excerpt)

```
//    Make a theme options page
function childtheme_add_admin() {
  global $childthemename, $childshortname, $childoptions;

  if ( $_GET['page'] == basename(__FILE__) ) {

    if ( 'save' == $_REQUEST['action'] ) {
      // protect against request forgery
      check_admin_referer('childtheme-save');
```

```
     // save the options
     foreach ($childoptions as $value) {
       if( isset( $_REQUEST[ $value['id'] ] ) ) {
         update_option( $value['id'], $_REQUEST[ $value['id'] ]  );
       } else {
         delete_option( $value['id'] );
       }
     }

     header("Location: themes.php?page=options.php&saved=true"); ❶
     die;

   } else if ( 'reset' == $_REQUEST['action'] ) {
     // protect against request forgery
     check_admin_referer('childtheme-reset');
     // delete the options
     foreach ($childoptions as $value) {
       delete_option( $value['id'] ); }

       header("Location: themes.php?page=options.php&reset=true"); ❷
       die;
     }
   }
   add_theme_page($childthemename." Options", "$childthemename Options",
➥'edit_themes', basename(__FILE__), 'childtheme_admin'); ❸
}
add_action('admin_menu' , 'childtheme_add_admin');
```

This code handles the submission of the options form, saving the options to the database if the form was submitted with the **Save changes** button, or resetting them if it was submitted with the **Reset** button.

As I said, most of this can just be used as is without modification. The numbered lines may need to be adjusted as follows, depending on your setup:

❶ This line is redirecting back to the options page after the options have been saved. In order to function correctly, it will need to contain a reference to the PHP file where your custom options are being created: in our case, that's **options.php**. Should your custom option functionality be contained in some other file, you'll need to change the highlighted part of this line.

❷ The same as above: replace **options.php** with the name of the file where your custom options are defined.

❸ This line is where the menu item is added to the WordPress dashboard, allowing users to access your theme settings form. The highlighted parameter is the name of the function that outputs the form itself. We'll be writing that shortly; just remember that if you give it a different name, you'll need to change this.

The last line is a call to our old friend `add_action`, which will ensure that our new function is called when WordPress is building its admin menu.

If you load your site's dashboard at this point, you should see a link to your Wicked Theme Options page in the Appearance menu, just above the Thematic Options link, as depicted in Figure 7.1.

Figure 7.1. A link to our options page in the Appearance menu

Clicking the link will result in an error. That's normal: we've told WordPress that our options page will contain the output of the `wicked_admin` function, but we've yet to write it! Let's do that now.

The Options Form

The last piece of the theme options puzzle is a form that will allow your users to select or enter the options they want. The code below is a general-purpose form builder, which I'll call the options form toolkit. It will loop over your `$childoptions` array and construct an appropriate form element for each one, pre-filling it with either the saved value if it exists, or the default value provided in `$childoptions` if it doesn't.

It's a big function, but there's nothing terribly complicated going on here. Because it can be used essentially without modification, I'll skip going over what every line does:

```
chapter_07/v1/wicked/library/options.php (excerpt)

function childtheme_admin() {

  global $childthemename, $childshortname, $childoptions;

  // Saved or Updated message
```

```php
  if ( $_REQUEST['saved'] ) echo '<div id="message" class="updated fade">
➥<p><strong>'.$childthemename.' settings saved.</strong></p></div>';
  if ( $_REQUEST['reset'] ) echo '<div id="message" class="updated fade">
➥<p><strong>'.$childthemename.' settings reset.</strong></p></div>';

  // The form
?>

<div class="wrap">
<h2><?php echo $childthemename; ?> Options</h2>

<form method="post">

<?php wp_nonce_field('childtheme-save'); ?>
<table class="form-table">

<?php foreach ($childoptions as $value) {

  // Output the appropriate form element
  switch ( $value['type'] ) {

    case 'text':
    ?>
    <tr valign="top">
      <th scope="row"><?php echo $value['name']; ?>:</th>
      <td>
        <input name="<?php echo $value['id']; ?>"
               id="<?php echo $value['id']; ?>"
               type="text"
               value="<?php echo stripslashes(get_option( $value['id'],
➥$value['std'] )); ?>"
        />
        <?php echo $value['desc']; ?>
      </td>
    </tr>
    <?php
    break;

    case 'select':
    ?>
    <tr valign="top">
      <th scope="row"><?php echo $value['name']; ?></th>
      <td>
        <select name="<?php echo $value['id']; ?>"
                id="<?php echo $value['id']; ?>">
          <option value="">--</option>
          <?php foreach ($value['options'] as $key=>$option) {
            if ($key == get_option($value['id'], $value['std']) ) {
              $selected = "selected=\"selected\"";
            } else {
```

```php
                    $selected = "";
                }
            ?>
            <option value="<?php echo $key ?>" <?php echo $selected ?>>
➥<?php echo $option; ?></option>
        <?php } ?>
        </select>
        <?php echo $value['desc']; ?>
    </td>
</tr>
<?php
break;

case 'textarea':
$ta_options = $value['options'];
?>
<tr valign="top">
  <th scope="row"><?php echo $value['name']; ?>:</th>
  <td>
    <?php echo $value['desc']; ?>
    <textarea name="<?php echo $value['id']; ?>"
              id="<?php echo $value['id']; ?>"
              cols="<?php echo $ta_options['cols']; ?>"
              rows="<?php echo $ta_options['rows']; ?>"><?php
      echo stripslashes(get_option($value['id'], $value['std']));
    ?></textarea>
  </td>
</tr>
<?php
break;

case "radio":
?>
<tr valign="top">
  <th scope="row"><?php echo $value['name']; ?>:</th>
  <td>
    <?php foreach ($value['options'] as $key=>$option) {
      if ($key == get_option($value['id'], $value['std']) ) {
        $checked = "checked=\"checked\"";
      } else {
        $checked = "";
      }
    ?>
    <input type="radio"
           name="<?php echo $value['id']; ?>"
           value="<?php echo $key; ?>"
           <?php echo $checked; ?>
    /><?php echo $option; ?>
    <br />
  <?php } ?>
```

```php
            <?php echo $value['desc']; ?>
          </td>
      </tr>
      <?php
      break;

      case "checkbox":
      ?>
      <tr valign="top">
        <th scope="row"><?php echo $value['name']; ?></th>
        <td>
          <?php
          if(get_option($value['id'])){
            $checked = "checked=\"checked\"";
          } else {
            $checked = "";
          }
          ?>
          <input type="checkbox"
                 name="<?php echo $value['id']; ?>"
                 id="<?php echo $value['id']; ?>"
                 value="true"
                 <?php echo $checked; ?>
          />
          <?php echo $value['desc']; ?>
        </td>
      </tr>
      <?php
      break;

      default:
      break;
    }
  }
  ?>

  </table>

  <p class="submit">
    <input name="save" type="submit" value="Save changes"
➥class="button-primary" />
    <input type="hidden" name="action" value="save" />
  </p>

  </form>

  <form method="post">
    <?php wp_nonce_field('childtheme-reset'); ?>
    <p class="submit">
      <input name="reset" type="submit" value="Reset" />
```

```
    <input type="hidden" name="action" value="reset" />
  </p>
</form>

<p><?php _e('For more information … ', 'thematic'); ?></p>

<?php
} // end function
```

Near the bottom of the snippet, there's a paragraph that you can edit to add some information about your theme, including links to your documentation pages.

With this code in place, our theme options page will now load without error; we'll see a form with all the options specified in our $childoptions array, as shown in Figure 7.2.

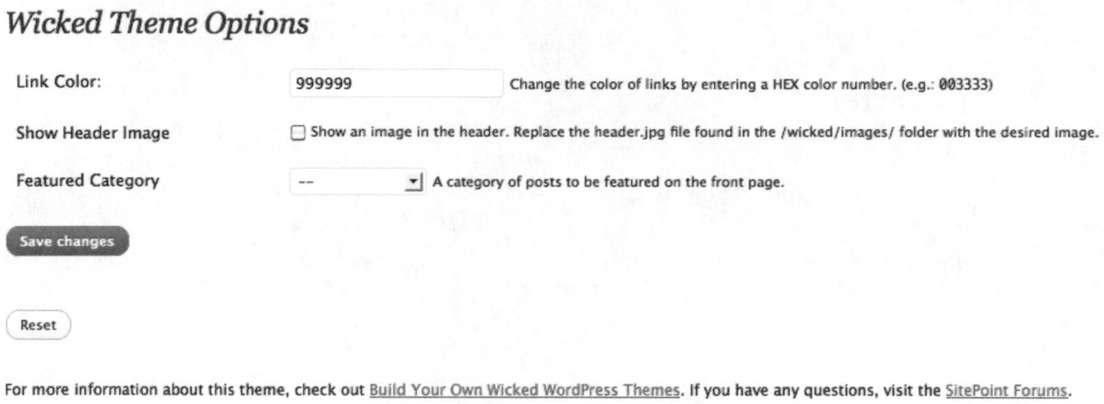

Wicked Theme Options

Link Color:	999999 Change the color of links by entering a HEX color number. (e.g.: 003333)
Show Header Image	☐ Show an image in the header. Replace the header.jpg file found in the /wicked/images/ folder with the desired image.
Featured Category	-- ▾ A category of posts to be featured on the front page.

[Save changes]

(Reset)

For more information about this theme, check out Build Your Own Wicked WordPress Themes. If you have any questions, visit the SitePoint Forums.

Figure 7.2. The final theme options page

Thanks to the toolkit, the only step required to add a new option to your theme is to add it to the $childoptions array. The construction of the form and all the communication with the WordPress database will be handled transparently. Go ahead: give it a try. Add a new option to your $childoptions array and watch it appear in the form, complete with save and reset functionality.

This options form toolkit also plugs into the default WordPress styling, so our options page blends in nicely with the rest of the WordPress dashboard.

Using Options in Your Theme

That was a lot of work, but it's paid off: we now have a flexible baseline of options page code that can be readily adapted to allow for any kind of options on any theme we develop. But how do we use those settings to modify the behavior of our theme? Fortunately for us, that part turns out to be much easier.

Altering CSS

In the options panel we created previously, we defined three options: one for link color, one to add a custom header image, and a third for selecting a featured category.

Of those three, the first two only require simple CSS changes, so we'll start with them. Our **options.php** file has grown quite large, and so far still serves a single purpose: defining our custom options form. To keep our theme code organized, let's put the options-dependent CSS code into a separate file, which we'll call **style-options.php** and include in **functions.php** as follows:

chapter_07/v1/wicked/functions.php *(excerpt)*

```php
// include style options
include('library/style-options.php');
```

The first task in this file is to load in the saved options, or the defaults if none have been saved. We'll start a new function, and do just that:

chapter_07/v1/wicked/library/style-options.php *(excerpt)*

```php
function wicked_load_custom_styles() {
  // load the custom options
  global $childoptions;
  foreach ($childoptions as $value) {
    $$value['id'] = get_option($value['id'], $value['std']);
  }
```

This is more boilerplate code: you can reuse it any time you want to load your theme options from the database. It dumps each option into a variable named after the option's id, so our `wicked_link_color` setting will now live in a `$wicked_link_color` variable.

The rest of this function simply needs to output the relevant CSS:

chapter_07/v1/wicked/library/style-options.php *(excerpt)*

```php
  // output a style sheet with the options
  ?>

  <style type="text/css">
    /* <![CDATA[ */
    /* Color Options */
    a, a:link, a:visited,
    #content a,
    #content a:link,
    #content a:visited {color:#<?php echo $wicked_link_color; ?>;}

    <?php if ($wicked_show_logo  == 'true') { ?>
```

```
    #blog-title {
      background: transparent url('<?php echo
➥get_bloginfo('stylesheet_directory') ?>/images/header.png') left top no-repeat;
      padding-left: 120px;
      height: 100px;
    }

    <?php } ?>

    /* ]]> */
  </style>

  <?php
} // end function
```

This part of the function spits out a `<style>` tag with our options handily included: we're echoing out the value of `$wicked_link_color` inside a rule, and testing for `$wicked_show_logo` to determine whether or not the **header.jpg** image should be shown.

To insert this `<style>` tag into our theme, we just have to hook the function into the `wp_head` action:

chapter_07/v1/wicked/library/style-options.php *(excerpt)*

```
add_action('wp_head', 'wicked_load_custom_styles');
```

With this in place, the output of our function will be injected into the document's head, dropping the styles right where they need to be. At this point, you should already be able to change your theme's link color and header image (assuming you have a **header.jpg** file in the **images** directory). Sweet, eh?

Altering Markup

That example only used options to modify CSS. The same thinking can be applied to changing markup. Thanks to Thematic's great hooks and filters, it's extremely simple to change your theme's output based on settings defined in the options form. For example, let's say when we turn our show header option on, we want to add a `class` attribute to the blog title `div`.

Here's how you could accomplish this:

chapter_07/v2/wicked/functions.php *(excerpt)*

```
function remove_thematic_blogtitle() {
  remove_action('thematic_header','thematic_blogtitle',3); ❶
}
add_action('init','remove_thematic_blogtitle');
```

```
// In the header div
function wicked_blogtitle() {
  // load the custom options
  global $childoptions; ❷
  foreach ($childoptions as $value) {
    $$value['id'] = get_option($value['id'], $value['std']);
  }

  if('true' == $wicked_show_logo) { ?>
    <div id="blog-title" class="header-image"> ❸
      <span><a href="<?php bloginfo('url') ?>/"
              title="<?php bloginfo('name') ?>"
              rel="home"><?php bloginfo('name') ?></a></span>
    </div>
  <?php } else {
    thematic_blogtitle(); ❹
  }
}
add_action('thematic_header', 'wicked_blogtitle', 3); ❺
```

Here's a breakdown of what's going on in the code:

❶ First, we'll remove Thematic's default `thematic_blogtitle` function from the header. As usual, this requires a function hooked into `init`.

❷ These few lines are the same code we've been using to load in the custom options as individual variables. They should be looking familiar by now!

❸ If `$wicked_show_logo` is set, we'll output some custom markup. This was copied from the `thematic_blogtitle` function we're replacing, in order to stay consistent. The difference is the `class="header-image"` we've added to the `div`.

❹ If, on the other hand, `$wicked_show_logo` _isn't_ set, we'll fall back on the standard `thematic_blogtitle` function.

❺ Finally, we add our custom title function to the header, with the same priority as the Thematic function we removed to make sure it's at the same place.

This is a simple example, but you can see how you could apply this principle to change any aspect of your theme's markup based on user-defined settings.

Altering Functionality

Now for the featured category. Back in Chapter 4, Raena showed you how to customize the front page to display only the four most recent posts in a magazine-style layout. Well, now that we're allowing our users to select a featured category, let's pick four posts from our featured category only.

This is actually quite easy. In **functions.php** we have a function called `wicked_indexloop`, whose job it is to display the custom home page Loop. At the top of that function, begin by adding the standard code to load the custom options:

```
function wicked_indexloop() {

  // load the custom options
  global $childoptions;
  foreach ($childoptions as $value) {
    $$value['id'] = get_option($value['id'], $value['std']);
  }

  query_posts("posts_per_page=4");

  ⋮
```

Now it's simply a matter of modifying the `query_posts` call to include a category parameter:

```
function wicked_indexloop() {

  // load the custom options
  global $childoptions;
  foreach ($childoptions as $value) {
    $$value['id'] = get_option($value['id'], $value['std']);
  }

  query_posts("posts_per_page=4&cat=" . $wicked_feature_cat);
```

Now if you select a category in your options page, the front page will display only posts of that category. Impressive.

Adding Color Variants

We've seen how we can allow users to input their own custom colors for the theme, which can work for some basic background or highlight colors. But what if you want to fully skin your theme in a number of different colors, or using decorative images and multiple shades?

The process will be fairly similar, though this time we'll want to write full style sheets for each variant and add them to the page conditionally. Let's start by creating a new directory in our theme folder, called **skins**. In it we'll make three other folders, called **red**, **yellow**, and **blue**. Each of those folders will contain a **skin.css** file and a **header.png** file.

For the purposes of illustration, we'll keep our style sheets as simple as possible, containing only the same few color rules we used above. It goes without saying, however, that the sky's the limit in terms of what you can put in your variant style sheets. Here's our **blue.css** file:

/chapter_07/v3/wicked/skins/blue/skin.css

```
a, a:link, a:visited {
  color:#0033FF;
}
#blog-title {
  background:transparent url('header.png') left top no-repeat;
}
```

The red and yellow stylesheets are similar:

/chapter_07/v3/wicked/skins/red/skin.css

```
a, a:link, a:visited {
  color:#FF0000;
}
#blog-title {
  background:transparent url('header.png') left top no-repeat;
}
```

/chapter_07/v3/wicked/skins/yellow/skin.css

```
a, a:link, a:visited {
  color:#FFFF00;
}
#blog-title {
  background:transparent url('header.png') left top no-repeat;
}
```

The Options Form

Now we need to modify the theme options form to display a selection of color variants. To do this, we simply update the `$childoptions` array in our **options.php** file as follows, replacing our link color and header image options with a new array for the color variant option:

chapter_07/v3/wicked/library/options.php *(excerpt)*

```
function childtheme_options() {
  global $childthemename, $childshortname, $childoptions;

  ⋮

  // the color variants array
  $color_variants = array(
```

```
    "blue" => "blue",
    "red" => "red",
    "yellow" => "yellow"
);


$childoptions = array (

  array( "name" => __('Color Variant','thematic'),
         "desc" => __('Select which color scheme or variant you
➥would like to use.','thematic'),
         "id" => "wicked_color_variant",
         "std" => 'blue',
         "type" => "radio",
         "options" => $color_variants),
  ⋮
```

This will create a form on the theme options page that looks like the one in Figure 7.3.

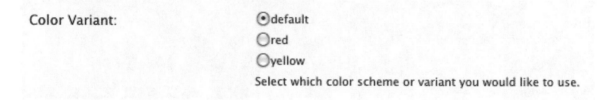

Color Variant: ⦿ default
                     ◯ red
                     ◯ yellow
                     Select which color scheme or variant you would like to use.

Figure 7.3. A radio button selection for the color variant

Adding the Style Sheets

Next, you'll have to add the selected style sheet to your `head` so that the styles appear on the site.

WordPress has a function for adding style sheets dynamically, called `wp_enqueue_style`. It allows you to keep track of versions, and specify the loading order and dependencies. It's called `wp_enqueue_style` because it places the style sheets in a queue before adding them to the document, so it can do all that extra processing. As an example, here's how we'd add our blue style sheet:

```
wp_enqueue_style(
  'wicked-blue', // Style ID
  get_bloginfo('stylesheet_directory') . '/skins/blue.css', // Path to stylesheet
  '', // dependencies (empty)
  '', // version (empty)
  'all' // media attribute
);
```

Now we just update our `wicked_load_custom_styles` function, in **library/style-options.php**, to enqueue a style sheet based on the option selected. Cut out the `<style>` tag output from that function, and replace it with a call to `wp_enqueue_style`, so that it looks like this:

```
chapter_07/v3/wicked/library/style-options.php (excerpt)
```

```php
function wicked_load_custom_styles() {
  // load the custom options
  global $childoptions;
  foreach ($childoptions as $value) {
    $$value['id'] = get_option($value['id'], $value['std']);
  }

  wp_enqueue_style('wicked-skin', get_bloginfo('stylesheet_directory') .
➡'/skins/' . $wicked_color_variant . '/skin.css', '', '', 'all');
} // end function
```

It's quite simple: we're just inserting the $wicked_color_variant option into the style sheet path string.

Our style sheet has to be enqueued *before* the head of the document is rendered, so we're unable to hook into wp_head as we did before. Fortunately, WordPress has an action hook called wp_print_styles for just this purpose:

```
chapter_07/v3/wicked/library/style-options.php (excerpt)
```

```php
add_action('wp_print_styles', 'wicked_load_custom_styles');
```

With this in place, you should be able to select a color variant and have the appropriate style sheet loaded on the front end. Now you just need to flesh out those skins with some fancy CSS of your own!

Custom Page Templates

When you create a page in WordPress, you may specify a custom template for it on its editing screen. This template will override the usual WordPress page template hierarchy entirely.

Why might you want to use a specific template? Perhaps you'd like your site to feature a few landing pages that omit all that distracting bloggy stuff, like the sidebars, menu, or footer. You might like to create a special type of archive display, or show a list of all your blogroll links. For those of you who plan to release themes to the public, providing a bunch of templates for common purposes is a real deal-sweetener.

To build a custom page template, you first need to create a new file for it in your child theme's root directory. Let's say we want to create a page template specifically designed for a company to present its mission statement. We'll call our file **mission-statement.php**.

A page template must start with a single comment, beginning with the words `Template Name:`, like this:

```
chapter_07/v4/wicked/mission-statement.php (excerpt)

<?php
/*

Template name: Mission Statement

*/

⋮
```

Even with just that comment in place, our template will already show up in the Page Attributes panel when editing a page, as shown in Figure 7.4.

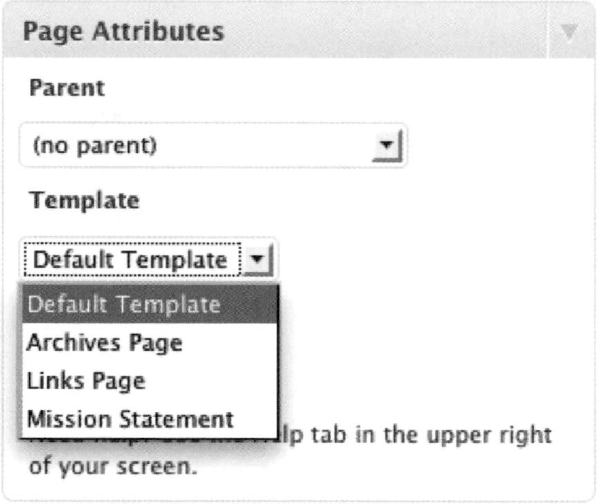

Figure 7.4. Our new Mission Statement template in the **Page Attributes** panel

Of course, because our template file is empty, only a blank page will be displayed when you view a page that's been set to use this template.

What you put in your template file is entirely up to you, though you should probably include the page content to avoid confusing your users! Because so many plugins rely on the `wp_head` and `wp_footer` action hooks, you should make sure to include these as well. In Thematic, these are called in **header.php** and **footer.php** respectively, so including those files with `get_header` and `get_footer` will serve you well. Beyond that, you can put in whatever widget-ready areas, markup, and Loops you want.

Thematic includes two custom page templates in addition to its default **page.php** file: **archives.php** (the Archives Page template) and **links.php** (the Links Page template). Have a look at those three files, and consider using one of them as the starting point for your own page template.

For our Mission Statement template I have gone with Thematic's **page.php** file, except that I've commented out the call to `thematic_sidebar`; the page will be uncluttered and allow the site's mission statement to stand on its own. I've also removed `thematic_postheader`, so the page's title won't be displayed—just the mission statement itself will appear:

chapter_07/v4/wicked/mission-statement.php (excerpt)

```
// creating the post header
//thematic_postheader();

⋮

// calling the standard sidebar
//thematic_sidebar();
```

To make the content span the full width of the page—to compensate for the missing sidebar—we'll revisit the home page style from way back in Chapter 5:

```
body.home #container {
  float: none;
  margin: 0;
  width:960px;
}
body.home #content {
  width:900px;
  overflow:hidden;
  margin: 0 0 0 10px;
}
body.home .hentry {
  width: inherit;
}
```

As you might have come to expect by now, Thematic provides you with a handy `body class` based on the template the page is using. View your page's source to see it in action:

```
<body class="wordpress blogid-1 y2010 m06 d22 h03 singular
  slug-about page pageid-2 page-author-admin page-comments-open
  page-pings-open page-template page-template-mission-statement-php
  loggedin mac fircfox ff3">
```

Copy your home page styles and modify them to refer to that `class`. While you're at it, make the text nice and big:

```
chapter_07/v4/wicked/newstyles.css (excerpt)

/* =Mission statement template styles
------------------------------------------------------------- */
body.page-template-mission-statement-php #content {
  width:900px;
  overflow:hidden;
  margin: 0 0 0 10px;
}
body.page-template-mission-statement-php .entry-content {
  font-size: 1.8em;
  line-height: 1.2em;
}
body.page-template-mission-statement-php .hentry {
  width: inherit;
}
```

With that, your users will have access to a specially crafted page template to display their mission statements. As always, much of the value will be a result of the attention you give to the page's custom CSS, so have at it!

Shortcodes

Another simple, yet powerful way to give your users more control over the theme is through a technique that WordPress calls **shortcodes**. Shortcodes are like widgets, except that they can be added directly to the content of posts using a predefined code. You may already have experience with WordPress shortcodes if you've used the gallery or video embedding codes built into WordPress versions 2.9 and up.

For example, Figure 7.5 shows how to embed a gallery shortcode into a post, and Figure 7.6 shows how the gallery displays on the site (this assumes, of course, that images are added to the post's image gallery).

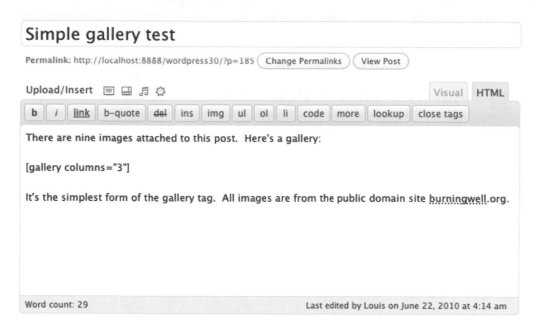

Figure 7.5. The gallery shortcode in a post

There are nine images attached to this post. Here's a gallery:

It's the simplest form of the gallery tag. All images are from the public domain site burningwell.org.

Figure 7.6. The resulting gallery display

The principal benefit of shortcodes is that they allow your users to add content with specific styles and markup that may be beyond their own abilities to produce. If you have a simple shortcode that produces the desired result, all you need to do is give them a few examples of how to use it.

Building Your Own Shortcodes

WordPress has a shortcode API that makes building your own shortcodes extremely quick and easy. For this example, we're going to create a shortcode to create pullquotes. The rich-text editor in WordPress already includes blockquote functionality, but we'll enhance ours a little: it will allow users to optionally define the width and cite the author of the quote—all with only a few lines of code.

Here's how the markup will look in our HTML:

```
<blockquote class="pull-quote">
  <p>Maecenas ante nisi, placerat … </p>
  <cite class="author"> &mdash; Allan Cole</cite>
</blockquote>
```

Now technically, a user could insert this markup on their own in the WordPress back end using the HTML editor. However, imagine how tedious it would be to hand code the markup each time, let alone add the correct classes without constantly making mistakes. Shortcodes help to make this a quick process—a major benefit to the general user who'll often be afraid of code.

We'd like our users be able to type this instead:

```
[pullquote width="400" author="Allan Cole"]Maecenas … [/pullquote]
```

Much like HTML, WordPress shortcodes can have opening and closing tags: these will allow you to manipulate the content between the tags in interesting ways.

To add our custom shortcode, we simply need to create a function that accepts two arguments: `$atts`, which will be the options provided to the shortcode, and `$content`, which will be the content between the opening and closing shortcode tags.

We first extract the attributes in `$atts`, providing some defaults; then we return the desired output, including the provided content and attributes as required:

```
                              chapter_07/v5/wicked/functions.php (excerpt)

function pull_quote_sc($atts, $content = null) {
  extract(shortcode_atts(array(
          'width' => '600',
          'author' => '',
          ), $atts));
  if (!$author == '') {
    $authorname = '<cite><em>' . esc_attr($author) . '</em></cite>';
  } else {
    $authorname = null;
  }
  return '<blockquote class="pull-quote" style="width=' . esc_attr($width) . '">
    <p>' . $content . '</p>' . $authorname . '</blockquote>';
}
```

The last step is to call the WordPress `add_shortcode` function, passing it our shortcode's name, as well as the function we want to provide the shortcode's content:

```
                              chapter_07/v5/wicked/functions.php (excerpt)

add_shortcode("pullquote", "pull_quote_sc");
```

The last step is to define some CSS for the pullquote. We've added a `class` called `pullquote` to our `blockquote` element, so that we can style it specifically and separately from the default `blockquotes` that may already be present in your content.

Here are some basic styles to start with:

```
                              chapter_07/v5/wicked/newstyles.css (excerpt)

blockquote.pull-quote {
  border-left: 1px dotted #CCC;
  padding: 5px 0 5px 20px;
}

blockquote.pull-quote cite {
  display: block;
  text-align: right;
}

blockquote.pull-quote cite:before {
  content: "—";
}

blockquote.pull-quote p {
  font-size: 1.5em;
  line-height: 1.1em;
}
```

The final output of the shortcode is shown in Figure 7.7.

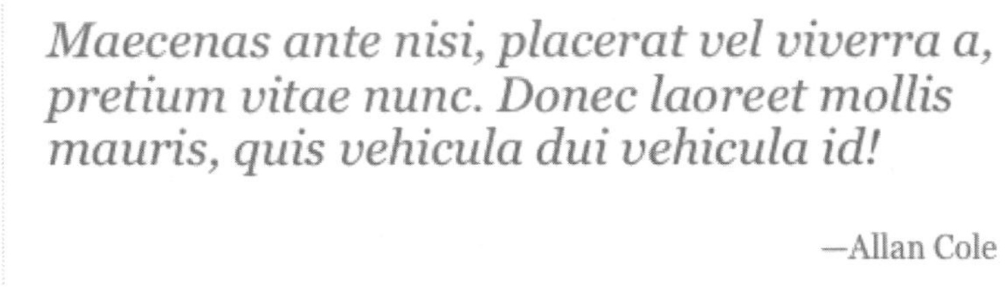

> *Maecenas ante nisi, placerat vel viverra a, pretium vitae nunc. Donec laoreet mollis mauris, quis vehicula dui vehicula id!*
>
> —Allan Cole

Figure 7.7. The fully styled pullquote displaying on the front end

Customizable Menus

WordPress 3.0 introduced powerful functionality in the form of the wp_nav_menu function. This function—which Brandon briefly touched on in Chapter 2—allows end-users to customize their site's menu using a simple tool in the WordPress dashboard. The latest version of Thematic has been updated to take advantage of this functionality, though it's not enabled by default; if it was, it might break older child themes that had been developed based on the traditional page list menu.

To enable customizable menus in a Thematic child theme, all we need to do is add a filter to the thematic_menu_type hook, and return 'wp_nav_menu':

chapter_07/v6/wicked/functions.php *(excerpt)*

```php
function wicked_change_menu_type() {
  return 'wp_nav_menu';
}
add_filter('thematic_menu_type', 'wicked_change_menu_type');
```

With this code in place, you can now create a custom menu in the dashboard's **Appearance** > **Menus** page, then select it in the **Primary Menu** drop-down to have it appear in place of the page list menu. This gives users the power to fully customize their site's navigation menu with an arbitrary selection of categories, pages, or any other links they want. Given how little code is required to set this up, it's a feature you should definitely consider adding to your theme.

You can even add extra menus to your theme, so that users will be able to customize each menu separately. Let's take a stab at doing that. Two steps are required: first we need to register the menu, then add it to our template(s).

Registering the menu is easy—just call register_nav_menus with an array containing your menu's ID and its name:

chapter_07/v6/wicked/functions.php *(excerpt)*

```php
register_nav_menus(array('secondary' => __('Secondary Menu')));
```

Now, when you view the Menus administration area in the dashboard, you'll have an extra drop-down for the secondary menu. But, as we haven't added it to any of our templates, any menus that users put there won't be displayed. To fix that, we just call wp_nav_menu in our template. Let's add it above the primary sidebar:

chapter_07/v6/wicked/functions.php *(excerpt)*

```php
function wicked_secondary_menu() {
  wp_nav_menu(array('theme_location' => 'secondary','fallback_cb'=> ''));
}

add_action('thematic_abovemainasides', 'wicked_secondary_menu');
```

We now have access to another menu location, and any links added to it will appear above the sidebar. Booyah!

With Great Power ...

Now that you have a good grasp on the different types of optional features you can add to your theme, you should be mindful of how you intend your options to be used—especially when you're distributing themes.

Here are a few points to consider:

■ What will the workflow be like for my users when adding content that requires them to interact with custom-built options? Is that process simple and clear?

■ Is a similar option already built into WordPress or Thematic? How can I tap into that option so that I'm not repeating functionality?

■ What happens if a publisher uses one of my features incorrectly? Will it break the theme, display an error message, or do nothing?

The rule of thumb here is to always consider how users will interact with your theme. While your primary goal is to make your options powerful and robust, making them simple and enjoyable to use runs a close second.

Selling Your Theme

by Jeffrey Way

So, you've built a gorgeous, usable, robust, and customizable theme. Now what? It's time to take it to market! As designers and developers, it can be difficult to make the shift into becoming salespeople for the stuff we build, so this chapter is intended as a guide to the world of selling WordPress themes.

It's a common misconception that, because WordPress—and consequently, any themes developed on top of it—is bound to the General Public License (GPL), designers are unable to profit from selling them. Luckily, this is far from the truth—as I'm sure you've already guessed from the very existence of this chapter.

We'll start by deconstructing this myth, and move into what you can do to make your theme more attractive to buyers, finally touching on the mechanics of selling themes.

Understanding the GPL

The GPL, or General Public License, is the license under which WordPress is distributed. Thematic is also GPL-licensed, as are a number of JavaScript libraries you might be including in your theme (such as jQuery). A full copy of the GPL is located in your WordPress installation directory, in the file **license.txt**. It's a bit intimidating—a large file with a smattering of legal terms—but it's worth a read if you're interested in understanding the license terms in depth.

For the less legal-minded among you, I'll provide a quick breakdown. According to the Free Software Foundation[1]—a nonprofit organization that promotes free and open source software—the GPL allows for four freedoms:

- the freedom to use the software for any purpose

- the freedom to change the software to suit your needs

- the freedom to share the software with your friends and neighbors

- the freedom to share the changes you make

> "When a program offers users all of these freedoms, we call it free software."
> —The Free Software Foundation[2]

Free software? This is what causes the most confusion among theme designers. Fortunately, in this case, free does not mean free, at least not in the way you might think. Free in the context of free software refers to *freedom*, not to price. Nothing in the GPL says that I'm forbidden from charging for my software. As a WordPress theme developer, I have the freedom to charge for my templates. That said, the buyer of my theme must also be provided with the GPL's freedoms to modify and redistribute this same work—for free if they want.

> WordPress, itself, wouldn't exist if it weren't for the freedoms afforded by licenses like the GPL.
> —Matt Mullenweg

Let's break this concept down into an example that's easy to understand. Bindy is a WordPress theme designer who wants to begin profiting from his designs. However, he read in a blog post that WordPress themes should be bound to the general public license. After a quick Google search, he uncovers numerous paragraphs stating that any potential buyers of his theme would also acquire the freedom to modify and/or share the theme any way they wish. As such, Bindy associates the word freedom with free, and ultimately decides to pursue other ventures.

This experience is all too common, and one that I receive emails about on a weekly basis. However, Bindy's chain of thought is perfectly understandable: licensing terms really are confusing—especially for us right-brain, who-needs-instructions designers!

Had Bindy performed just a bit more research, he most definitely would have come across the plethora of marketplaces that offer premium WordPress themes, with prices ranging from twenty-five to a few hundred dollars.

---

[1] http://www.fsf.org/
[2] http://www.gnu.org/licenses/quick-guide-gplv3.html

So how is this possible? How are designers like Bindy able to sell multiple copies of the same WordPress theme, when buyers technically have the freedom to redistribute the template however they see fit? The answer to this question is multifaceted.

You're Not Only Selling the Theme

As you complete your incredible, feature-filled WordPress template, it might be easy to forget that, once it's listed on your favorite marketplace, you're selling more than just the theme's files.

Support

Like it or not, one of the things you're selling when you sell a premium theme is knowledge, or, as a buyer might refer to it: support! In fact, support is often the key difference between free WordPress themes and premium offerings. This might seem superfluous at first glance to you as a (by now!) highly skilled theme developer, but it's important to remember that your target audience isn't made up of coders—quite the contrary, actually. A huge percentage will consist of business owners, photographers, bands, and perhaps enthusiastic bloggers who were a bit too inspired by the movie *Julie and Julia*. I assure you that, to these individuals, quality support is far from superfluous.

Along with your theme, you're selling your expertise. Why would a small business owner download a free template when they could instead pay thirty dollars and be assured that if they have any problems, the author (and a solution) is only an email away? Do not underestimate the importance of this selling point.

Documentation

In fact, assuming your template performs moderately well, you might find that providing support is a full-time job. For this very reason, it becomes essential that you automate as much as possible.

When ready to begin selling your template, your first step is to prepare the necessary documentation for it. While this is certainly tedious, if you fail to do it at the start, you'll be doomed to answer the same questions over and over. As such, do yourself a favor and cover anything and everything in your documentation.

Once your documentation is ready, the next step is to proceed under the assumption that your buyers won't read a single word of it. All joking aside, this unfortunately proves to be true more often than not. Consider preparing email form autoresponders for your buyers; note that this will also entail setting up a specific email account for support, perhaps, support@mysite.com. This way, when you receive a support request, an email will automatically be sent out to to the buyer, notifying them that you'll be in touch as soon as possible, but that you have also included a collection of frequently asked questions and answers for their convenience.

If this feels too informal to you, you should at least prepare some email templates to use when replying to support requests. Even if you edit them slightly for each response, it will save you from RSI!

Video Tutorials

To add yet another layer of convenience and support for buyers, many template authors go as far as creating short video tutorials to add that extra touch for those who prefer a more hand-holding approach. Online services, like Screenr,[3] make the process of recording short screencasts as easy as it can possibly be.

Screenr, which launched in 2009, is a Twitter-integrated screencast recording and hosting site. The advantage over other hosts, such as YouTube, is that no screencast software is required; it's built in. You only need to log in, press record, and Screenr will do the rest! Note that videos are, at the time of writing, limited to five minutes in length.

Convenience

When I was a kid, my favorite part of going on a school field trip was the boxed lunches that each child received at lunch time. There was no specific food component that stood out; rather, it was the simple fact that I received a little package that always excited me. I think this proves true for most people. We've established that there's more to selling a WordPress theme than just the actual product, so we must then consider additional selling points. Case in point: convenience.

The goal with any service is to provide a logical and, more importantly, simple buying experience. Businesses live and die according to their execution of this philosophy.

When preparing your theme, one monetization option is to sell it on your own website—perhaps your portfolio or blog. This is actually quite common. Why pay some marketplace a percentage of every sale, when you can soak in 100% of the profits? Ask yourself, "Does this conform to my proposed philosophy?" Is it convenient for a small business owner to have to visit your personal website and follow your custom purchasing guidelines? Better yet, ask yourself, "As a buyer, would it be more convenient to purchase a template from a designer's personal site, or a reputable theme marketplace that probably offers cheaper prices?" Ultimately, the question is: What offers the most convenience for the buyer?

With this knowledge in mind, you'd be remiss to not consider choosing a high-quality marketplace as the headquarters for your offerings. It's important to remember that your craft is design, not marketing. While a percentage from every sale will go to the marketplace, the added exposure your template will receive should far outweigh any losses in profit. Most importantly, it's convenient for buyers when they can visit an established marketplace, and be assured that their purchase has been reviewed and conforms to the highest standards on the Web. Convenience is key.

---

[3] http://screenr.com/

Dual Licensing

Let's be honest here: any moderately successful template, for any language and framework, can be obtained somewhere for free, most likely via BitTorrent. Piracy is simply a cost that must be factored into the equation, no matter how many additional services you provide to your paying customers. While it does help to send takedown notices to sites like RapidShare, you'll never win this battle.

However, when it comes to WordPress, you need to ask yourself if this is even a battle you want to fight. Are you adhering to the terms of the GPL if you prohibit these freedoms? Remember freedom #3: "The freedom to share the software with your friends and neighbors."

With this knowledge of our theme's inherited license, whether or not it's "pirated" becomes moot, as that distribution is explicitly permitted by the terms of the license. For this very reason, some theme marketplaces never send takedown notices: it flies in the face of the GPL's intention as they see it.

Regardless, takedown notices *are* sent by some theme marketplaces, such as the site I managed for two years, ThemeForest. So how can they technically do this?

WordPress themes from ThemeForest are sold with dual licensing. This is possible because, though all PHP code that hooks into WordPress's functions must inherently be bound to the GPL, this is not necessarily true for the CSS and JavaScript.

> So a theme—the CSS, images, and JavaScript—might be separate but the actual PHP code that generates a theme uses WordPress functions … so theme PHP needs to be GPL.
>
> —Matt Mullenweg

As such, on ThemeForest, every WordPress template is sold with two licenses:

- one for the WordPress code—that is, all of the PHP
- another proprietary license for the JavaScript and CSS files

In truth, typical buyers don't take the time to understand the licensing terms. While this might initially be disconcerting, in reality it needn't be. Most small business owners or bloggers have no desire to redistribute your files on the Web, nor would they even know how to. Their primary goal is to create a working dynamic website—nothing more. However, for those who wish to redistribute a theme, a dual license would only allow them to do so with the WordPress code. Because themes are invariably distributed in their entirety, this affords the marketplace the legal right to send takedown notices to these sites.

It's important to note that every WordPress marketplace handles licensing in its own unique way. It's up to you to research the terms for each marketplace when deciding on your home base. You should also take some time to consider what you personally feel most comfortable with. That might be to go 100% GPL and trust that customers will be attracted by the convenience and added benefits of buying from you, or it might be a more restrictive dual licensing scheme.

Whichever licensing option you decide on, you still face the challenge of encouraging buyers to consider your theme. The rest of this chapter will focus on marketing your theme effectively.

What Makes a Theme Sell?

So you've developed an attractive blog theme using WordPress, and are hoping to take it to the next level and profit from your work. Here's the hard truth: excluding a sale here and there, the market is minimal for nice, generic WordPress blog themes. Such themes are widely available for free around the Web. Nevertheless, some theme creators make a very good living from their WordPress designs. To successfully prepare a premium quality template, it's essential that you first study what makes certain themes stand out. Otherwise, you'll find yourself running with the pack, and in this highly competitive market, that's worth avoiding at all costs.

Multiple Color Schemes

Everything else being equal, what incentive is there for a potential buyer to choose a template offering one color scheme over a similar template with ten? The answer, of course, is that there's none. Allan showed you how to provide color scheme options in the last chapter; it might be tedious (after all, you're essentially designing the same theme five or ten times over), but it's convenient for the buyer, and that can often make the difference between a few sales and a few hundred.

Brandon, who sells his themes on ThemeForest under the user name epicera,[4] uses color options as a major selling point for his designs, and has found significant success in doing so. The various color schemes of his Flex theme are shown in Figure 8.1. By adding this extra layer of convenience for buyers, his templates consistently outsell those of his peers. Still, not one to sit idly, he also includes a plethora of features with every template, including custom fonts and an extensive admin panel.

Much like Brandon, the ThemeForest user Webtreats[5] offers an impressive ten color options in his successful inFocus template. The theme was a huge success, generating over $50,000 in sales in barely two months. As with all aspects of life, the little things are what make the biggest differences. While a buyer with a modest level of CSS knowledge could feasibly create their own color variation of a purchased theme in an hour or so, why should they? You are the designer; it's your job to make the buyer's life as easy as possible.

---

[4] http://themeforest.net/user/epicera
[5] http://themeforest.net/user/webtreats

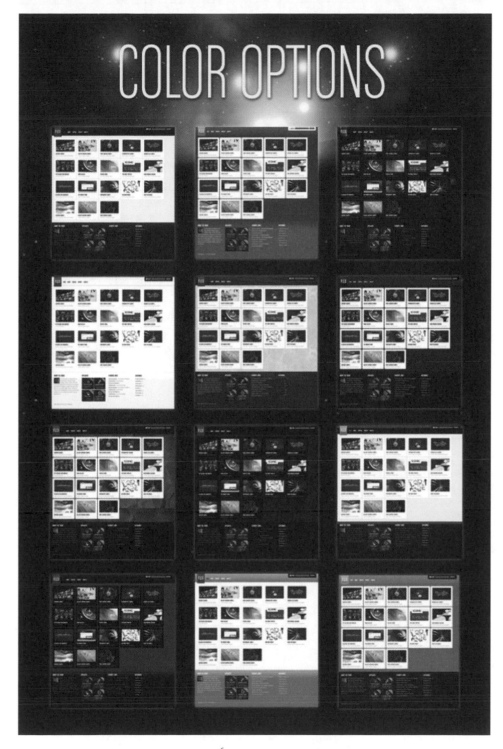

Figure 8.1. Brandon's Flex Theme[6] offers an impressive 12 different color schemes

Custom Configuration Options

Some authors expect a buyer to manually edit the PHP files when a simple change is requested. For instance, "How can I replace the stock logo with my company logo?" or "How can I change to the blue color scheme?" Most of the time, this is the wrong approach. A good rule of thumb is to always design for the lowest common skill level.

Never assume that a buyer will even understand what PHP is, let alone how to edit the code and upload it to the server. This is where the custom theme options you learned about in Chapter 7 come into play.

The WooThemes custom admin framework makes the process of configuring each of the themes a breeze. Among other options, the dashboard—shown in Figure 8.2—allows users to select their preferred style sheet, add a custom logo, and set banner images. By investing this time into building a helpful framework for the buyers, WooThemes further consolidates itself as a fantastic marketplace.

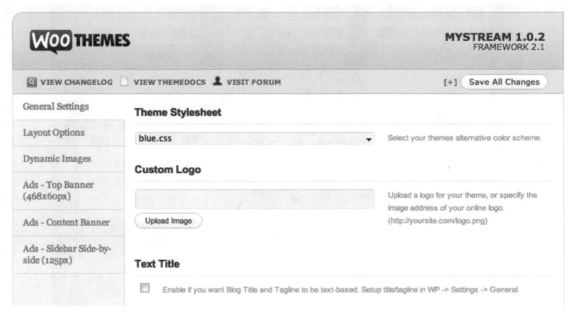

Figure 8.2. WooFramework2 is included with all the WooThemes WordPress themes

Freebies

Who says there's no such thing as a free lunch? Talented designer Dany Duchaine[7] offers the source Photoshop (PSD) files of his various themes for free. As such, he gains recognition and builds his brand, while also directing sales to the coded up HTML and WordPress versions of his themes. His site is shown in Figure 8.3.

---

[7] http://freepsdtheme.com/

Figure 8.3. Dany Duchaine's site FreePSDTheme

The smartest template authors don't just send their themes into cyberspace and wait for the sales to come in. They actively and creatively promote their items on a daily basis. It's a full-time job for them.

Embracing the Latest Technologies

The best template designers are quick to embrace the latest techniques and tricks, whether they come in the form of a new jQuery slider or the latest additions to the WordPress framework itself. This means that they read numerous RSS feeds daily, and are first in line to beta test the latest versions of WordPress. By doing so, they can be quick out of the gate with a new template boasting the latest features.

Image Sliders

Web template designers are well aware of the latest trends—and boy do they come and go! In late 2009, a wonderful Flash slider called CU3ER[8] burst onto the scene, and proceeded to generate a considerable amount of buzz in the template community. We're all chipmunks: if it's shiny with bells and whistles, it stands to reason that we'll respond with "Ooohh!"

Quickly following the release of this Flash slider, the very talented Christian Budschedl (also known on the web as Kriesi[9]) released his latest theme, and it just so happened to feature CU3ER. That theme, called Display[10] and shown in Figure 8.4, went on to become one of the best-selling WordPress themes on ThemeForest.

This is «display», a unique Themeforest template for showcasing your work and perfect for any business in need of a stunning website...

Figure 8.4. The Display theme, by Christian Budshcedl, featuring the CU3ER slider

These days CU3ER is less widely used in the template community, due to some licensing changes in early 2010 that limited redistribution rights. As such, many designers have recently moved on to the excellent Nivo[11] alternative.

Nivo is particularly nice because it mimics the sliding effect found in CU3ER and other similar Flash sliders, but it does so with jQuery!

When adopting any new bells and whistles, it's important to first determine whether you're really embracing new technologies, or just following a trend that will soon lose its appeal.

---

[8] http:// www.progressivered.com/cu3er/

[9] http://themeforest.net/user/Kriesi

[10] http://themeforest.net/item/display-3-in-1-business-portfolio-wordpress-/74542

[11] http:// nivo.dev7studios.com/

Custom Fonts

Up until recently, designers were forced to choose from only a handful of web fonts when designing their sites or templates. While you can use Arial or Georgia in your WordPress theme—and in some cases they might be the best tool for the job—it's essential that you take advantage of the latest tools and techniques.

It's almost laughable now, but as little as two years ago, we were using Flash (sIFR) to display text using custom fonts … *Flash*! In its defense, it truly was the best option available at the time, and we were grateful for it. Luckily, thanks to cufón,[12] `@font-face`, and other technologies and services, integrating a beautiful typeface is now a much simpler task.

Take the Google Font Directory, for example; after making a font selection from the catalog,[13] you only need to link to a Google-hosted style sheet and set your CSS `font-family`, accordingly. That's it!

So, for example, the following code will produce the output shown in Figure 8.5:

```
<!DOCTYPE html>
<html lang="en">
<head>
  <meta charset="utf-8">
  <title>Custom Fonts in 30 Seconds</title>
  <link href="http://fonts.googleapis.com/css?family=Lobster"
➥rel="stylesheet">
  <style>
    body { font-family: 'Lobster', serif; }
  </style>
</head>
<body>
Hello World
</body>
</html>
```

Figure 8.5. The Lobster font from the Google Font Directory

---

[12] http://cufon.shoqolate.com/generate/
[13] http://code.google.com/webfonts

At the time of writing, Google's Font Directory only offers around a dozen curated custom fonts. Though this number will surely increase over the course of time, if you require a unique font that's unavailable, it only takes an extra moment or so to write the `@font-face` rules yourself.

That said, font licensing is a tricky and confusing subject. Often you'll find yourself traversing through page after page, trying to decipher if the amazing font you found can be distributed with your theme. In these cases, I've found that it's far easier to utilize the `@font-face` kits from the wonderful Font Squirrel[14] site.

Font Squirrel offers `@font-face` "kits," which contain everything you need to use the fonts straight away, and they've done their homework: the fonts there are free and licensed for use in commercial projects. Keep in mind that, of course, the service is unable to guarantee 100% that the licensing terms for each font have been interpreted correctly. With that said, if they did make a mistake, they'd be notified about it rather quickly.

Mobile Browsing

As mobile browsing continues to increase in popularity, you might like to consider also offering a mobile-optimized style sheet. By doing so, you not only offer more convenience for the buyer, you also gain another selling point to add to your list of features.

Mobify[15] allows you to easily create a new style sheet specifically for mobile browsers. While this task can be accomplished manually, Mobify greatly simplifies the process.

Another avenue you might want to investigate is David Kaneda's excellent jQuery plugin jQTouch,[16] which allows a website to make use of the iPhone and iPod Touch functionality—such as swipes or orientation changes. This plugin has found considerable success in the community; in fact, the 2010 jQuery conference in San Francisco made use of jQTouch for the mobile version of its website.

Keep It Simple, Student

Clean, professional, and simple is key when it comes to WordPress theme design. Consider the theme in Figure 8.6.

This template has generated over $45,000 in sales in roughly ten months. Though the design is visually quite simple, it's the detail that makes it such a big seller: multiple color schemes, numerous widgetized regions, child themes, custom CSS for popular plugins, custom fonts, and the list goes on. By keeping the design simple and appealing to the masses, the author, vfxdude, has enjoyed considerable success.

---

[14] http://www.fontsquirrel.com/
[15] http://mobify.me/
[16] http://www.jqtouch.com/

BigFeature

HOME   EXAMPLE PAGES   DOCUMENTATION

Introduction to the theme

JUNE 18, 2009 | DOCUMENTATION, GENERAL, VIDEO | 6 COMMENTS

BigFeature is a flexible theme with Content Based Design. CBD is when the articles themselves changes the look of the site, with feature images and big headlines. Another important thing that this theme got that makes it a true CBD is that the rest of the design is simple and clean, with no distracting elements to take away the focus of the content. Adding a lot of space between elements is also essential to move to the next generation of CBD.

› Read More

Vimeo video test

NOVEMBER 5, 2009 | VIDEO | NO COMMENTS

From version 1.3 videos can be added to posts like default images…even thumbnails are produced. The supported external video sites are Vimeo, Youtube, Google Video, Dailymotion, MySpace, Veoh, Youku and uploaded video files. › Read More

FEATURED POSTS

Changelog
01/04/2010 • The new features and bug fixes to the new releases of BigFeature are listed here. Version 1.3.4 (just released) Improved the bfthumbs more

Figure 8.6. The BigFeature[17] theme, developed by vfxdude

Pull In the Reins and Solve Problems

A visually stunning theme is no guarantee of sales going through the roof; the best selling templates *solve problems.*

You can build a neat motorcycle-flavored template, chock-full of as many chrome textures as you can manage, but if it fails to appeal to a wide range of people—and it will—why bother? For better or worse, when designing for a marketplace, pull in the design reins a bit and appeal to the masses; you'll be thankful when the sales start rolling in!

When managing ThemeForest, I was often emailed about why my particular marketplace lacked more specialized templates. For example, why were there no themes tailored for bowling alleys? The answer, of course, is that there was nothing hindering authors from submitting such themes; but as a theme designer, why would you invest a significant amount of time into a template that would only appeal to a small percentage of people? There's absolutely a market for highly specialized themes, but these sorts of designs might be more appropriate on a per-client basis, as a freelancer.

Test, Test, Test

It goes without saying that releasing your first commercial WordPress theme is exciting! But don't let this overshadow the need for thorough testing. If you're audacious enough to launch an untested theme to the public, you'll only harm your reputation and make further sales difficult.

Browser Testing

Does the theme display correctly within the most popular browsers? As of June, 2010, StatCounter Global Stats reports the following usage statistics:[18]

Firefox	31.1%
Internet Explorer 8	27.7%
Internet Explorer 7	15.6%
Internet Explorer 6	9.6%
Google Chrome	8.8%
Safari	3.0%
Opera	1.6%

---

[17] http://themeforest.net/item/bigfeature-wordpress-theme/51702

[18] http://gs.statcounter.com/#browser_version-ww-monthly-200905-201006

If you code with web standards in mind, browser compatibility generally is a small issue—at least when it comes to the modern browsers. If a theme displays correctly in Google Chrome, you can rest assured that it will most likely render similarly in Firefox and Safari. However, it's a different scenario when it comes to Internet Explorer 7, and IE6 is another story altogether.

Should you compensate for Internet Explorer 6 at all? With 10% of the market share and falling, is it worth your time? There is no definitive answer to this question. What type of template are you building? Does it have a target—and perhaps more youthful—audience (such as a theme for bands)? If so, chances are that you won't need to worry about IE6. On the other hand, if you're building a more generalized theme, how important will those visitors be to your potential buyers? I'd wager "very!" Do your homework, and make up your own mind on this issue; however, I'd encourage you to take a few extra hours to add support for this decade-old browser. For personal projects, I don't touch IE6 with a ten-foot pole. But for commercial themes, we just have to roll up our sleeves and hold our noses.

Plugin Testing

It's smart practice to test each newly developed theme with a handful of the most widely used WordPress plugins. While there are literally thousands available, there are a few standout plugins that are too popular to risk ignoring:

- All in One SEO Pack: http://wordpress.org/extend/plugins/all-in-one-seo-pack/

- Google XML Sitemaps: http://wordpress.org/extend/plugins/google-sitemap-generator/

- Contact Form 7: http://wordpress.org/extend/plugins/contact-form-7/

- NextGEN Gallery: http://wordpress.org/extend/plugins/nextgen-gallery/

Once you begin developing your own customized baseline for each new theme, this step will become quicker as you'll be more familiar with potential pitfalls; however, play it safe—at least at first—and take a few moments to test-install these plugins.

Educating the Community

When it comes to generating profits from your designs, it's interesting to note that the process is far more involved than you might initially think. While purchasing banner ads and AdSense keywords on Google are smart practices, this isn't a business that can simply be placed on autopilot as you throw money at various advertising venues—nor should you want it to be! You must be an active participant.

Consider giving back to the WordPress community, whether it be in the form of participation in forums, or even writing articles for various tutorial sites. You can be paid for the article itself, and you'll gain the benefit of a link back to your site, as well as an improved reputation as a WordPress designer.

Your first thought after reading the above paragraph might be "Hey—I'm a designer, not a writer." That may be so, but you're also an expert in your field—or at least on your way to becoming one! There's monetary value in that. You don't have to be a flawless technical writer—that's what the editors are for. As long as you write reasonably well, and see yourself as an educator, you should have nothing to worry about.

While writing a tutorial does not specifically direct traffic to your themes, if done regularly it can massively boost your name in the community. Besides, you can sporadically use your themes as examples in your tutorials. So you're able to promote your portfolio and your name, while educating and providing a service to the community. Just show a little modesty when referencing your own designs!

Three Avenues for Selling Your Themes

You should perform a significant amount of research when determining where and how to sell your themes; this is an extremely important decision, and not to be taken lightly.

While there are numerous ways to promote yourself and your portfolio, when it comes to actually generating revenue from your templates, you generally have three options.

One Website Per Theme

Perhaps the most traditional of the three options, it's not uncommon to build a website specifically for the purpose of selling a single theme. While this is still quite a popular method for selling themes, it's also the most time-consuming, and can be inconvenient for buyers.

Ask yourself, "How often will I build new WordPress themes?" If you're hoping to turn this into a business, consider the ramifications of a tailor-made website for every new theme:

■ How will you cross-promote when you've launched your second theme?

■ Will each new theme receive a customized website, or will you use the same skin? If the former, is that a good use of your time? Would it be better spent working on new designs?

■ Once you've managed to build a dozen templates or so, how will it affect your business? At that point, would it be smarter to build a full marketplace?

While it might initially be quicker to take the "one website per theme" route, think about where you want to be a year from now, and let that guide you.

Your Own Marketplace

The next logical step is to launch your own marketplace, similar to WooThemes, RocketTheme, Elegant Themes, and plenty of others.

Many of these sites are subscription based, meaning that buyers aren't paying specifically for one template. Instead, a yearly subscription grants them access to every template in the catalog.

It's important to note that, generally speaking, a subscription-based model will appeal more to freelance coders than to those who are simply in need of an attractive business template for their company. In the latter case, the term "subscription" is less of a selling point and may even scare them away. After all, they're already going to be paying monthly for web hosting; why would they want to pay a subscription just to use a theme?

If you choose to sell themes individually—which is the most common method—there are several considerations that must be taken into account.

Licensing

What licensing structure will you choose? GPL? 100% proprietary (which Matt Mullenweg often refers to as "evil")? A combination of both, perhaps, as discussed previously? I would personally recommend against a proprietary license, as this really does fly in the face of the spirit of WordPress.

How will the theme be used?

Equally important is the need to consider how your theme will be used. Will this have an effect on how much you charge? For example, consider two buyers: John and Jane. John simply wants a new skin for his blog. Jane, on the other hand, intends to redistribute the theme as a freebie in her monthly web magazine publication.

With this knowledge, is it fair for both John and Jane to pay the same amount? Depending on your license choice, maybe not. If your theme is fully GPL-licensed, then the discussion is moot, because you're unable to restrict either buyer's right to redistribute your theme. On the other hand, if your theme is dual-licensed, you might consider offering both single-usage and more expensive extended licenses.

Single-usage license
> As the name suggests, a single-usage license should grant buyers the right to use your theme once, for one project. This essentially means that they could use your theme for client X's project, but should they require this theme—even a modified version—for client Y the following month, the buyers would then need to purchase an additional license from you.

Extended-use license, also called a developer license
> There will be times when a buyer requires more flexibility than a single-usage license permits. This is why it's important to also offer an extended agreement option; though it should come

with a significant price increase. While you're free to modify this ratio, it's most common in the community to go with a figure along the lines of 50:1, or possibly 25:1. So, if buyers purchase a $50 theme, but select the extended license, they'll pay somewhere between $1,250 and $2,500. Some marketplaces include additional incentives with extended licenses. This may consist of premium support, or source PSDs to make modifications easier for developers.

When would such a license be purchased? Imagine if a team developing a new content management system want to purchase your theme and adapt it for use with their CMS. They then intend to offer it as a free theme to their community. In this instance, potentially any member of their community could download and use your theme.

Extended licensing terms vary from marketplace to marketplace, and can ultimately be molded according to your needs and preferences. With this much variation and potential complexity, it's generally a best practice to offer an FAQ or guide to explain the licensing terms to your buyers. If this stuff is confusing to you, imagine how bewildering it might be for the average small business owner!

Confusions could arise if the buyer incorrectly assumes that purchasing an extended license affords them the right to do practically anything they wish with your theme. This is most often not the case. Generally, extended licenses will still fall under a per-project basis. Referring back to our CMS example from above, if the makers choose to build a different CMS a year down the road, they would not have permission to continue using your theme for that second project. Most extended licenses allows for implementation and/or redistribution of a theme for *one* project.

Choosing an Existing, Reputable Marketplace

You might also find that you're not as interested in the business aspect of selling your themes. You're a designer, not a marketer, after all. If you fall into this category, it's probably best to focus exclusively on designing, and leave the specifics—payment gateways, promotion, reviewing—to a third-party marketplace such as ThemeForest.

Soaking It All Up

When all is said and done, making a living as a WordPress theme designer is a full-time job—but, one with many rewards! Your stature in the community will increase, profits are automated and roll in daily, and perhaps most importantly, you're able to do what you love for a living! What's better than that?

Index

What now?

So, you've mastered the fine art of building WordPress themes. What's next on your repetoire?

Why not expand your horizons beyond reliance on WordPress' prebuilt widgets and plug-ins?

With *jQuery: Novice to Ninja* you'll learn to build the functionality you need from scratch - from custom widgets to interactive forms to dynamic menus and more!

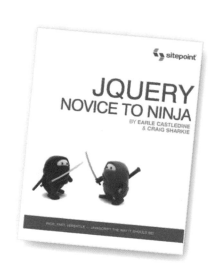

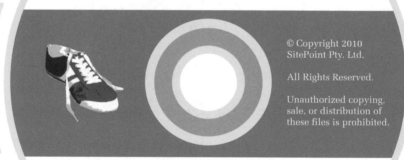

BUILD YOUR OWN
WICKED WORDPRESS
THEMES

CODE ARCHIVE

No, the CD-ROM is not missing.
Download all of the files used in this book from:
http://www.sitepoint.com/books/wordpress1/code.php